ECONOMIC DEVELOPMENT OF BOSNIA AND HERZEGOVINA DURING AUSTRO-HUNGARIAN PERIOD

COMPARATIVE ANALYSIS OF MACROECONOMIC INDICATORS

BY

TAHIR MAHMUTEFENDIC

Gotham Books

30 N Gould St.
Ste. 20820, Sheridan, WY 82801
https://gothambooksinc.com/

Phone: 1 (307) 464-7800

© 2023 *Tahir Mahmutefendic*. All rights reserved.

No part of this book may be reproduced, stored in a retrieval system, or transmitted by any means without the written permission of the author.

Published by Gotham Books (December 22, 2023)

ISBN: 979-8-88775-682-0 (H)
ISBN: 979-8-88775-680-6 (P)
ISBN: 979-8-88775-681-3 (E)

Because of the dynamic nature of the Internet, any web addresses or links contained in this book may have changed since publication and may no longer be valid.

The views expressed in this work are solely those of the author and do not necessarily reflect the views of the publisher, and the publisher hereby disclaims any responsibility for them.

REVIEWERS

Professor Vjekoslav Domljan

Moenes Mahmutefendic, BA, MA, Cert. ACC

ACKNOWLEDGMENTS

I owe a debt of gratitude to the following individuals:

Moenes Mahmutefendic for editing the book and useful comments

Enita Corovic for help and support

Professor Vjekoslav Domljan for supplying valuable resources and for useful advice

Staff of the National and University Library of Bosnia and Herzegovina for invaluable help in providing the literature

CONTENTS

ACKNOWLEDGMENTS iv

LIST OF TABLES vi

PREFACE... ix

INTRODUCTION xiii

CHAPTER ONE

    THE LAST DECADES OF OTTOMAN RULE IN BOSNIA .. 1

CHAPTER TWO

    AUSTRO-HUNGARIAN INTEREST IN BOSNIA AND HERZEGOVINA... 21

CHAPTER THREE

    LITERATURE ON THE AUSTRO-HUNGARIAN PERIOD IN BOSNIA AND HERZEGOVINA.................................... 39

CHAPTER FOUR

    METHODOLOGY... 67

CHAPTER FIVE

    SECTORAL ANALYSIS OF THE ECONOMY OF BOSNIA AND HERZEGOVINA... 73

CHAPTER SIX

    ECONOMIC DEVELOPMENT OF BOSNIA AND HERZEGOVINA IN A COMPARATIVE PERSPECTIVE .. 169

CONCLUSION 183

APPENDIX ONE – SEVEN DECADES OF "FREEDOM" 189

APPENDIX TWO – ASSESSMENT OF YUGOSLAVIA 201

LITERATURE 216

LIST OF TABLES

Table 1 – Structure of agricultural land in Bosnia and Herzegovina

Table 2 – Average annual yields in production of various agricultural products in chosen countries 1889-1903

Table 3 – Number of various animals in Bosnia and Herzegovina in 1879

Table 4 - Bosnia and Herzegovina, sectoral agricultural production 1879 – 1914 (million crowns, prices in 1910)

Table 5 - Revenue from indirect taxes in Bosnia and Herzegovina 1885 – 1913 in crowns

Table 6 - Production of coal in Bosnia and Herzegovina in 1913

Table 7 - Production of coal, its value, and the number of workers (1885-1913)

Table 8 - Production of iron ore in Vares mine

Table 9 - Production, number of workers, and the value of production of manganese, chromium, copper, and mercury

Table 10 – Production of salt in quintals and the number of employees in saltworks in Bosnia and Herzegovina in a period 1905 – 1913

Table 11 – Production and its value and the number of employees in Zenica and Vares ironworks

Table12- Rise in export sales and value of wood from Bosnia and Herzegovina 1898-1911

Table 13 – Exports of dried plums from Bosnia and Herzegovina 1905-1918

Table 14 - Tobacco factories in Bosnia and Herzegovina

Table 15– Bosnia and Herzegovina 1881-1915: Value-added index of a big industry (all sectors 1907 = 1000)

Table 16 - Average annual growth rates in mining, railways, manufacturing industry, agriculture, and a foreign trade in Bosnia and Herzegovina during the Austro-Hungarian period

Table 17 - National product per capita in different territories in 1910 in $ in 1970

Table 18 - Relative Levels of GDP per Capita Countries Relative to the West European Average

Table 19 - Indexes of GDP per capita of Bosnia and Herzegovina and the chosen countries in 1910/1913, where the latter are given index 100

Table 20 - Revenue from indirect taxes in Bosnia and Herzegovina 1885 – 1913 in crowns

Table 21 - Population in Bosnia and Herzegovina in a period 1879-1910

Table 22 - GDP Per Capita in Successor States of Former USSR in 1990 (1990 international dollars)

Table 23 – GDP Per Capita in Successor Republics of Former Yugoslavia in 1990 (1990 international dollars)

Table 24 – Levels of Per capita GDP in European Countries, Annual Estimates for 1990 (1990 international dollars)

Table 25 - GDP per capita index for Bosnia and Herzegovina for 1910/1913 and 1990 compared to the chosen countries where the latter are given index 100

Table 26 – GDP levels and growth in Yugoslavia, its most developed parts, and chosen countries 1950-86 (in $ US)

Table 27 – GDP Per Capita Growth Rates in the Most Important Western European Countries and Yugoslavia 1950-73

PREFACE

Many Europeans do not live in the state in which they were born. There are people who lived in eight different states without changing their home address. Turbulent European history, full of violence, revolutions, and wars, has caused abrupt changes in state borders, national sovereignty, and political systems. In Eastern Europe there are two fields for analysis; the comparison of the achievements of capitalist and communist systems, and the comparison between the state of independence, and the state in which national sovereignty was lost.

The Yugoslav historians, almost in unison, talk about cruel and oppressive colonizers, who ruthlessly exploited natural resources of their colonies, and who were alienated from the people and their vital interests. Michael Palairet calls this "the Yugoslav myth".

The first Croatian president Franjo Tudjman in one of his speeches said "....that finally in freedom we overcome centuries-long backwardness". The Yugoslav lands, including Croatia, fared better, i.e. lagged less behind the West before World War I than before the break-up of Yugoslavia (Welfens). Serbia, Bulgaria, and Greece fared better, i.e. lagged less behind the West when they were the parts of the Ottoman Empire, than after gaining independence (Markovic). Would this be a sufficient reason to corroborate the former Austro-Hungarian Foreign Minister Gyula Andrassy's statement, that the Slavs are not fit to rule themselves and that they should be ruled by someone else?

Not necessarily! Czechoslovakia fared better in terms of economic development and political freedoms after the break-up of the Habsburg Monarchy. The most convincing explanation for the Slavic countries was offered by Mijo Mirkovic in his doctoral dissertation defended in Frankfurt in 1925, entitled "The Main Causes of Economic Retardation of the Slavic Nations". He claims that there are only minor racial differences between Germans and Slavs. The explanation of the relative backwardness of the Slavic countries Mirkovic finds in the Weberian thesis. He divided all the Slavic countries into the three groups; 1. Christian Orthodox countries, 2. Catholic countries, and 3. Predominantly Catholic countries, which experienced a partial Reformation. The Christian Orthodox countries are the least developed, while the Czech Republic, the Slovak Republic, and Slovenia, which belong to the third group, are the most developed. (Mirkovic)

There are many examples of the countries which fared better in terms of economic development when they were colonies than when they gained independence. It is conventional wisdom that the British were the best of all the bad guys - with the exception of their behavior in Ireland, where they conducted a cruel, Spanish-style colonial policy. In spite of this, Ireland grew faster than the Great Britain in the century before they gained independence. The average annual growth rate of its economy was 1.23 per capita between 1820-1913, compared to 0.89% for the Great Britain, reaching 55% of the British GDP per capita (Maddison). After thirty years of independence the Irish GDP per capita fell to 48% of the British GDP per capita. One needs to bear in mind that Ireland was neutral in the World War I, while Britain suffered destruction and human and material losses.

The Netherlands fared better when it was a Spanish colony. Poland experienced faster economic growth when it was carved-up between Austria, Prussia, and Russia. Is this sufficient reason to exclaim:" Long-live colonialism!?" Finally, the whole Enlightenment - from Kant to Hume, Voltaire, John Stuart Mill, and Marx - celebrated colonialism and glorified its "civilizing mission". The most fanatical advocates of colonialism, Marx and Engels, were ready to greet the British conquest of India, and the American annexation of California, and even slavery in the South of America before the Civil War, as a *condition sine qual non* of overcoming backwardness and promoting civilization

(Mahmutefendic, http://juventudnacional-min.blogspot.co.uk2011_08._01 archive.html)

Again, the answer is, not necessarily. When Finland was part of the Russian Empire it was a middle-income country. Nowadays, Finland tops the Human Happiness Index.

Everything boils down to the question: "Who are the colonizers, and who are the colonized?" In other words, at which level of economic, cultural, and civilization level are the colonizers and the colonized?

In the case of the Austro-Hungarian Empire, we are dealing with an economically, culturally, and civilizational advanced country occupying a backward and underdeveloped country. Occupying and liberating at the same time. Liberating from ignorance, backwardness and primitivism.

When assessing the achievements of the Austro-Hungary in Bosnia and Herzegovina, and comparing them with the achievements during the period of independence, one needs to bear in mind that different sources of data were used. This inevitably causes inconsistency. For example, Jackson (Jackson in Petrakos & Totev) and Maddison give Hungary and the Czech lands index 60 to the Western European average in 1913, while from Palairet's data Hungary's index was 70, and the index of the Czech lands was almost 95. The index of Bosnia and Herzegovina to the Yugoslav lands, ranges from 138 to 175. Montenegro's GDP was multiplied by 6 to adjust the price levels in 1910 and 1970. However, Kimberley Amadeo (Amadeo) estimates that $100 in 1910 was worth $386 in 1970.

While cardinal values are questionable, ordinal values are undisputable. Before the World War I Bosnia and Herzegovina was more developed than Greece and Russia, and at the same level of development as Italy. It was less developed than

Slovenia, Istria, Vojvodina, and Dalmatia, at the same level of development as Croatia proper with Slavonia, and more developed than Serbia, Kosovo, Montenegro, and Macedonia. In terms of population, 25% of inhabitants of the Yugoslav lands have higher GDP than inhabitants of Bosnia and Herzegovina. Before the break-up of Yugoslavia, all the non-Yugoslav countries were far more developed than Bosnia and Herzegovina. Bosnia and Herzegovina were more developed than Kosovo, and slightly more developed than Macedonia. In terms of population, 85% of inhabitants of Yugoslavia had a higher GDP than inhabitants of Bosnia and Herzegovina.

More than sufficient evidence to break "the Yugoslav myth".

INTRODUCTION

This book consists of six chapters and two appendixes. The first chapter analyses the last decades of Ottoman rule in Bosnia and Herzegovina. The aim of this chapter is to acquaint the reader with the economic situation in the country before the occupation. Agriculture was the main economic activity employing more than 90% of inhabitants of Bosnia and Herzegovina. A replacement of the *timar* system, which was more favorable to landless peasants compared to the Western feudalism, with a *chiftlik* system, led to a significant deterioration in the position of the peasant. Neither the peasants nor the landowners were motivated to invest in agriculture. As a result of unresolved agricultural issues, productivity lagged far behind Serbian and Bulgarian agriculture. Apart from agriculture, other industries included mining, forestry, banking, and transport, all of them undeveloped and in a rudimentary form. A particularly difficult situation was as regards to transport, where conditions were worse than in the medieval period. In the 1860s a charismatic governor, Topal Osman Sherif Pasha, put a lot of effort in modernizing Bosnia and Herzegovina. He built the first railway, schools, libraries, two hospitals, a printing house, and established a telegraph line between Sarajevo and Istanbul. In spite of his noble efforts, however, Bosnia and Herzegovina remained a country with a pastoral economy, extremely backward and undeveloped.

The second chapter deals with the interest of Hungary and Austria for Bosnia and Herzegovina. The Hungarian interest in Bosnia dates back to a medieval period, when the country was considered a vassal territory of Hungary. The Hungarian interest did not cease even with a Turkish conquest of the country in 1463. The Hungarians tried to establish two counties, one in Srebrenica, and one in Jajce, and to renew a shrinking Bosnian vassal state, with Nikola of Ilok as its king. After being decisively defeated by the Turks at the battle of

Mohac in 1526, and after the Austrian king Ferdinand became the Hungarian king, the Austrians took over their involvement in Bosnia from the Hungarians. However, a defeat against the Turks in 1737 delayed the Austrian's involvement in Bosnia's destiny for a century and a half. A decisive twist occurred in 1866 when the Austrian army was defeated by the Prussian army at the battle of Sadova/Konigratz. This marked a definite exclusion of Austria from the unification of Germany. The year after, a Compromise (Ausgleich) was struck with Hungary, which transformed the Austrian empire into Austro-Hungary. The interest in Bosnia, which laid dormant for centuries, was suddenly revived. It was materialized with the Congress in Berlin in 1878, where it was decided that the empire occupies Bosnia and Herzegovina and introduces its administration.

The third chapter gives a literature review on the Austro-Hungarian administration of Bosnia and Herzegovina. There is a voluminous literature which deals with the Austro-Hungarian period in Bosnia and Herzegovina. Many authors, domestic and foreign, historians, lawyers, political scientists, economists and physicians wrote either about certain aspect of this era, or analyzed the entire period. Most works were written by historians and economists. There is a significant overlap in their works. Historians could not avoid economic topics, while economists had to deal with historically relevant events. In the literature review the authors were divided into four groups: 1. Domestic historians, 2. Foreign historians, 3. Domestic economists, and 4. Foreign economists

This literature review leads to three conclusions:

1. Evaluation of the Austro-Hungarian period in Bosnia and Herzegovina ranges from extremely negative (Taylor) to extremely positive (Domljan).
2. With this exception, the evaluation of the foreign authors is more favorable compared to the assessment of the domestic authors.

3. More exact analysis, corroborated with facts and figures, results in a more favorable evaluation of the Austro-Hungarian rule in Bosnia and Herzegovina.

A fourth chapter is the shortest. It presents the methodology used in the following two chapters.

The authors, when discussing economic matters, use figures and numbers to corroborate their statements. These numbers are of two types; 1. physical such as the length of railway network, the number of KM of roads, production of agricultural and industrial goods, or the number of workers employed, and 2. Monetary such as the value of production, the level of foreign trade, the amount of banking capital or the level of workers' wages. However, apart from Palairet and Domljan, the authors do not use macroeconomic indicators such as GDP, GDP per capita, or rate of growth of GDP. These three indicators are vital in macroeconomic analysis. For with all its drawbacks GDP shows a size of an economy, GDP per capita the standard of living, while a rate of growth of GDP shows a dynamism of an economy and a success of economic policy measures. This is why in sectoral analysis of the Bosnian economy, these indicators will be used and, if not given calculated, provided that available data allow it.

Economic variables grow at an exponential trend, i.e. they increase by a geometric progression. This is why the formulae for doubling, tripling, quadrupling etc. of variables are derived and used. Also, logarithms are applied to calculate a growth rate of different sectors of the economy and the economy as a whole. In addition, formulae which involve powers are used to calculate the number of times of an increase in a certain variable over a period of time. Also, the relevant variables are discounted to adjust for changes in the level of prices.

Chapter Five deals with a sectoral analysis of the economy of Bosnia and Herzegovina. Agriculture was the dominant sector of the economy and it faced insurmountable problems because of unresolved ownership relations. The Christian Orthodox peasants, who accounted for the largest number of the serfs, hoped that the new Christian rulers would expropriate landowners and give them the land. This did not happen for three reasons; 1. The new administration did not want to alienate the Muslim landowners and turn them into enemies of the empire, 2. The powerful Hungarian landowners would not allow it since they were afraid that it could be a "dangerous precedence", and 3. The tithe was a very important source of the government revenue. As a result, agriculture lagged behind Serbia and Bulgaria, and grew at an average annual growth rate of less than 1%.

The new authorities gave a manufacturing industry a priority in economic development. The manufacturing industry was located mainly near the sources of raw materials and close to a transport network. The industrial policy was unwittingly a combination of a several economic doctrines, some of which did not exist at the time. The government would allow private enterprise to establish and then it would nationalize them. This strategy worked well in transport and a heavy industry, but was much less successful in a light industry. The manufacturing industry grew at a staggering average annual rate of more than 12%. However, the growth was regionally and sector unbalanced. As a result, many areas remained unindustrialized and unconnected by a transport network.

Chapter Six gives a comparative analysis of the development of the Bosnian economy. In-spite of imbalances and structural problems Bosnia and Herzegovina was more developed than Serbia, Greece, and Russia, and at the same level of development as Croatia proper with Slavonia and Italy. Before the World War I Bosnia and Herzegovina was the most developed Balkan country and in European relations it belonged to middle-income countries.

The first appendix, entitled "Seven decades of 'freedom'", deals with the position of Bosnia and Herzegovina in Yugoslavia. It is divided into two parts; the First Yugoslavia, and the Second Yugoslavia. In the First Yugoslavia, the position of Bosnia and Herzegovina deteriorated in absolute and relative terms. As a result, the country slipped below the Yugoslav average in terms of economic development. In the Second Yugoslavia Bosnia and Herzegovina was one of the six republics, i.e. federal units, and in theory was supposed to be equal with the other republics. In practice, Bosnia and Herzegovina was given the role of supplier of the products of base and extractive industry to more developed republics, which produced processed goods. The prices of the former were fixed, while the prices of the latter were freely formed in the market. This caused a transfer of value from Bosnia and Herzegovina to the more developed republics. As a result, the index of GDP per capita in Bosnia and Herzegovina compared to Yugoslavia slipped from around 150 to 66.

The second appendix assesses the achievements of Yugoslavia. The nineteen century romantic ideas about the single nation were replaced by politically more pragmatic Yugoslavism at the beginning of the twentieth century. The main reason of the creation of Yugoslavia was a threat of the other races. Politically, Yugoslavia was a successful project. During the first Yugoslavia, the territory of the South Slav lands was preserved. In addition, the victorious partisans added almost 20,000 square kilometers of the territory inhabited by the South Slavs by the end of the WWII. Economically, however, Yugoslavia was not successful. Not only did it not converge with more developed countries such as Greece, Italy, and Austria, but the difference in the level of development increased. When Yugoslavia was a political community, it was not an economic community. Now, although Yugoslavia is no longer a political community it is still a cultural community. Links in literature, arts, music, film, and theatre have been preserved even after the break-up of the country. Therefore, Yugoslavia was successful as a political and cultural project, but unsuccessful as an economic project.

CHAPTER ONE

THE LAST DECADES OF OTTOMAN RULE IN BOSNIA

INTRODUCTION

At the time of the conquest of the Balkans, which lasted from the middle of the fourteenth until the middle of the sixteenth century, the Ottoman state had structural features not different from the contemporary feudal states of Europe. The sultan was the overlord of powerful Turkish beys, who formed a virtual nobility.

The Ottoman landholding system, known under the name of *timar*, which was created from the middle of the fifteenth century until the last quarter of the sixteenth century, regulated agrarian relationships. The rights and obligations of the serfs, called *raya*, were laid down in detail in various documents such as provincial registers, land surveys and extant registers of judge (*kadi*) courts.

In accordance with the stipulations of the *timar* system, the individual peasant owned his house, barn, shop, vineyard, orchard, or vegetable garden. In the vocabulary of Roman law, the peasant's property was *dominium plenum in re potestam*, as the private property with all the rights it brings to the owner, namely *jus utendi, jus fruendi and* jus *abutendi* (the right to use, the right to collect yields and the right to sell). On the other hand, the agricultural land belonged to the state, and the individual peasant had only the right to use it. The individual peasant held the land in a perpetual lease, but was obliged to fulfil his obligations towards the cavalryman, called *sipahi*, who had the right to appropriate a certain amount of agricultural surplus as a compensation for his military service to the state (Adanir).

In addition, the peasant had to pay a land tax (*cift resmi* in the case of Muslims, and *ispence*, which was about 14% higher, paid by Christians). Both taxes substituted labor service, which previously was in place in the Ottoman system. Christian peasants had also to pay a household tax, which replaced a head tax (*cizye*), and which annually amounted to one Venetian ducat (Anadir).

Christians and Muslims paid to the treasury a tax on small animals like sheep and pigs, a very small amount. In addition to these taxes, which had a regular character, there were extraordinary, or irregular taxes (*avariz-i divaniyye*), levied upon fiscal units consisting of more households. The purpose of this tax was to support military campaigns. Privileged occupations were exempt from paying this tax. They included miners, rice cultivators, horse breeders, tar extractors, saline workers, producers of gunpowder, lubricating greases and oils and charcoal. According to some estimates, 13% of all households belonged to this privileged group, called *muaf* (Anadir).

The overall system of agricultural surplus extraction from the peasant, through tithes, paid to the sipahi, and various taxes, paid to the state, seems to be relatively light. As a result, the countryside enjoyed relative prosperity in the sixteenth century, resulting in demographic expansion. This trend coincides with similar developments in Europe, which also experienced agricultural and demographic upswings (Anadir).

Although the *timar* system was abolished only in 1831, it virtually ceased to exist two centuries earlier. It was gradually replaced by the *chiftlik* system, the system of large landholdings. A decisive factor which introduces radical changes in agricultural structure of the Ottoman state was the introduction of gunpowder, which replaced cavalrymen with infantry soldiers. As a result, the Janissary corps became the chief arm of the state. This infantry needed large estates as a source of food and military supplies and economic base of taxes collection, necessary to financially support war efforts.

Over a period of time, certain individuals managed to acquire large swathes of land, mainly on an extralegal basis. In this process, they became private property owners, which also included hereditary possessions. This transformation acquired different forms. A *chiftlik* owner might obtain leases from peasants, or he might also be a tax farmer and use this position to gain peasant holdings. This system had a great advantage because it could exploit economies of scales and increase production in order to meet increasing demand for food and raw materials in European countries (Jelavich).

The *chiftlik* system brought profound social and political changes and a shift in power between the central Ottoman government and provinces. The central power weakened significantly, while the power of mighty local Muslim landowners strengthened. These landowners, called *ayans*, were equivalent of the Christian notables in European countries. They were often agents of the central authorities in the local communities and performed various duties such as tax collection, the supervision of the land system, and maintenance of order. Their strength and power were enhanced particularly in the eighteenth century, when the central government of the Ottoman state was weakened by many disastrous wars. In addition, the *ayans* were able to organize their own private armies, whose numbers ran into thousands. These armies fought very often with the government forces and other local leaders and were used to control the peasants under control on the *chiftlik* estates (Jelavich).

This system led to a deterioration of the position of the peasants. Whilst in the timar system their obligations were fixed, predictable, and fairly light, they sharply increased in the *chiftlik* system. The peasants were left at the mercy of rapacious, greedy and insatiable local landowners, who usually dominated the political authority of the area and used armed guards to control those who worked land and to extract more and more of agricultural surplus. This was particularly pronounced in the most fertile lands, such as parts of Bosnia. In the mountainous and remote areas, individual peasants had more control over the land and herds, but they were subject to high taxes. In addition, uncertainty of tenure increased. They were at the mercy of those who held the political and police power in their region, and who milked them through various irregular and illegal dues (Jelavich).

The change in the system had a profound influence on the relationships between different religious groups in the Ottoman empire. Although an increased significance of the foreign trade, particularly exports to European countries, created a class of wealthy non-Muslim merchants and moneylenders, namely Greeks, Vlachs, Bulgarians, Serbs and Jews, nevertheless the vast majority of large landowners were Muslims, and peasants were predominantly Christians. Poor conditions often forced peasants to flee their land and seek protection of strong military leaders and eventually to join their forces. Increase in the number of brigands and outlaws added a fuel to the fire and spurred the insecurity and weakness of the state.

By the end of the eighteenth century, the Ottoman empire was exposed to three serious threats; the European powers, the unsatisfied Christian peasants, and the increasingly more powerful and independent *ayans*. The latter danger was the most ominous and threatened most to the integrity of the Porte. The situation was aggravated by the fact that *ayans* very often enjoyed support and sympathies from the local Muslim population. The state, therefore, had to take them into account and give them official positions. Also, because of the weakening might of the regular Ottoman army, the central power had sometimes to rely on the private armies of the *ayans*. In other to curb their power, the government tried to play the *ayans* against each other, who in turn supported antigovernment forces such as the rebellious Janissaries.

The problem of military weakness was recognized by the Ottoman rulers, who were well aware of the declining power of their state and urgent need to conduct deep reforms. There was a difference between those who thought that the major cause of the declining power of the state was the abandonment of the traditional principles, which guaranteed a glory for centuries, and those who considered old practices obsolete and outdated and therefore advocated modernization and Westernization of the state institutions (Jelavich).

REFORMS AND CHALLENGES

The first reforms were initiated by Sultan Selim III, who came to power in 1789. and who used an interlude of peace in 1792 to conduct profound reforms. Although the reforms were supposed to comprise many aspects of the Ottoman empire, such as the tax system and the administration system, the emphasis was on military reorganization. Even before Selim III came to power, French military instructors had been used, and the French government was willing to offer further support. The main weakness in the Ottoman military forces was the Janissary corps. This force became a separate political entity, more dangerous to integrity of the Ottoman empire than as an effective fighting force against serious foreign enemies. Selim's major accomplishment toward reform was the formation of a parallel and rival infantry, the Nizam-i Cedid, or the New Order, which received western style training and uniforms.

Unfortunately, Selim was not strong enough to complete reforms. The war with Russia and the uprising in Serbia weakened the central government, which enabled rebels to revolt and overthrow Selim III, and eventually kill him. A new regime was dominated by Muslim conservatives and Janissaries who opposed any reforms, fearing to lose privileged positions in the empire. Meanwhile, Selim's supporters and those who favored reforms gathered at Ruse in Bulgaria under the leadership of Mustafa Pasha. In 1808 these forces moved to

Constantinople and successfully brought Selim's cousin, Mahmud II to the throne and remained in power until 1838. (Jelavich)

Mahmud II became the first successful reforming sultan. However, he faced a strong resistance in various parts of the empire. A stiff opposition to reforms came mainly from local overlords, *ayans* and Janissaries. Three most powerful were Pasvanoglu Osman Pasha in Bulgaria, Ali Pasha of Janina and Mohammed Ali in Egypt. First two decades of the XIX century were characterized by frequently changed allegiances, disloyalty and false promises. The three powerful notables wavered between short-term loyalty to the central government and active participation in suppression of the rebellions throughout the empire and active encouragement of the rebel movements - particularly in Serbia, Bulgaria, and Greece (Jelavich).

Mahmud II decided to liquidate *ayans* and Janissaries, since their almost unrestricted power was the main impediment to reforms and centralization of the state. The sultan used the notorious and bloodthirsty Dzelal-Pasha to defeat the most rebellious *ayans* and Janissaries. After mass liquidations of Janissaries in their strongholds in Sarajevo and Mostar, the Sultan tried to make a compromise with *ayans*, whose services as well as those of the Janissary corps became superfluous. He offered them a position of *muteselims*, high-ranking civil servants in Ottoman administration. Ayans flatly rejected this offer, considering it humiliating to replace the lordship in their feudal fiefs with a position of a civil servant, albeit a respectable one. This paved a way to a direct arm conflict between the *ayans* and the central government (Imamovic).

The Bosnian vizier Ali Namik-Pasha Moralia tried again at the beginning of 1831 to convince the *ayans* to come to their senses and to accept reforms and loyalty to the sultan. Captains and *ayans* refused to go to Travnik to meet with the vizier. Instead, they gathered in Tuzla by the end of January. They agreed that they would reject newly proposed reforms, and to resist the introduction of the new army, new taxes, and secession of the three Bosnian's districts on the river Drina to Serbia. On the 5th February 1831, the *ayans* elected Husein-captain Gradascevic as their leader. After the Bosnian vizier in Travnik turned down the requests of the Bosnian *ayans* they clashed with the army of the grand vizier on the 18th July 1831 near Kacanik at Kosovo, in which Captain Husein Gradascevic scored a great victory. He was appointed the Bosnian vizier by the *ayans*, while Namik-Pasha Moralia fled to Herzegovina, and later via Dubrovnik to Istanbul. After that, the autonomy of Bosnia was declared in Sarajevo on 12th September 1831 (Imamovic).

The political program of the Bosnian *ayans* was not completely elaborated. The main points contained resistance to reforms, which according to them were against Islamic tradition, sanctity of their property rights, and requests that in the future the Bosnian vizier is recruited among native notables. This would virtually give Bosnia the same status of autonomous province which Serbia gained with *Hatiserif* in 1830. As regards the position of other layers of the Bosniak and non-Bosniak population, the program did not contain any changes. Contemporaries wrote that that Husein-captain Gradascevic as a "Dragon of Bosnia" was an intelligent and rich man, whilst a Franciscan chronicler, Jakov Baltic, claimed that the "Vizier Husein" treated Christians justly (Imamovic).

In-spite of this, the movement for Bosnian autonomy was mainly Muslim. It did not appeal to Christians, since it did not address their discrimination and subordinate position in the Bosnian society. Also, it had a strong religious connotation, since it referred to itself as "Turkish i.e Islamic (Hoare).

In-spite of this there is some evidence that Christians participated in the Husein's army. The Bosnian Orthodox Metropolitan allegedly contributed 6000 Christian troops to the struggle. Guardians of Franciscan monasteries also gave their support. Gradascevic also mobilized his Christian tenants into his army. Therefore, although the movement was primarily

Muslim, it contained elements of a wider Bosnian dimension, which encompassed the Christians (Hoare).

In a final showdown between the Sultan and Gradascevic's troops, a decisive role was played by the two Herzegovinian *ayans*, namely Ali-Aga Rizvanbegovic and Smail-Aga Cengic. They provided a vital aid to the sultan in a battle at Pale, near Sarajevo, on the 31st May 1832. The final resistance was crashed on the 4th June 1832, at the walls of Sarajevo. This defeat marked the end of the movement for the Bosnian autonomy. Rizvanbegovic was rewarded for his loyalty by detachment of the Herzegovinian *elayet* from the Bosnian *elayet*, which was given to him for government, with a title of Pasha. Sporadic rebellions lasted until 1850, when Omer-Pasha Latas eradicated the last vestiges of disloyalty to the sultan. In the process he killed Rizvanbegovic near Banjaluka, who naively thought that for the loyalty to the sultan he could survive the disappearance of the institutions of the *ayans* (Imamovic).

Although the movement for autonomy was suppressed, Bosnia was exempt from fringe reforms such as the introduction of a postal service, publication of an official newspaper, development of new schools and reform of ministries. But in 1839, Mahmud's son Abdul Mejid I replaced his father on the throne. He immediately introduced a set or reforms known as *Hatiserif of Dulhane,* (Solemn Charter in Rose Garden). This act gave all subjects in the empire the same status, regardless of their religion, with regards to personal security, civil rights, property and honor, thus abolishing *kanuni raya.* The reform envisaged new system of military recruitment and tax collection, which abolished the notorious practice of purchasing a right to collect taxes. These principles were further elaborated in the set of measures contained in a decree called *Hatihumajunu.* The whole set of reforms was called *tanzimat*, meaning reorganization of the empire, or in modern world terminology *perestrojka*. Principles espoused in *tanzimat* were well-intentioned, noble and well thought out. Unfortunately, the principles of *tanzimat* had a weak or no effect in remote parts of the empire such as Bosnia (Malcolm).

Weak implementation of the reform measures hit peasants in Bosnia the hardest. In the old *timar* system, which lasted until 1830s, peasants usually had a life tenancy. The landowner was allowed to expel the peasant only if he neglected his duties. They included payment of one tenth to the state and between one twelfth and one ninth of the crop, depending on local customs as well as some labor services. Before 1830s the peasant rarely paid more than one fifth of the crop (Palairet). In the *chiftlik*, system the peasant was reduced to the position of a sharecropper. "*His obligations both in labor and in dues in kind were significantly increased. Instead of being subject to fixed obligations, he was now at the mercy of the landowner, who usually dominated the political authority of the area and used armed guards to control the peasants who worked the land. In the mountainous and remote areas individual peasant families had more control over the lands and herds, but taxes were high and tenure sometimes uncertain. They were also at the mercy of those who held the political and police power in their region*" (Jelavich*)*.

The condition of the peasant in Bosnia was one of the worst in the Balkans. The peasant had to pay one tenth of the crop to the state and one third to the remains of the crop to the landowner. This amounted to 40% of the crop. One could say that the modern man in developed countries pays roughly the same amount in direct taxes and contributions. However, the modern man expects to get in return free health service, free education for children, state pensions, child benefit etc. On the other hand, a payment of mortgage instalments can swallow up 50% of a household income, while the landowner was obliged to provide a house for the peasant and his family and help him in repairing of his home (Malcolm).

The following paragraph shows the quality of the peasant's accommodation:

"The average peasant throughout the Balkans lived in an extremely simple mud, stone, wood, or brick home consisting usually of one or two rooms. His chief furniture was a small table and low stools; he and his family slept on blankets or on a raised platform. He cooked over a fireplace in his main room in clay pots using wooden utensils. In a rich village or house the furniture might be more complete and the floors covered with furs or richly decorated rugs. Here gaily embroidered pillows, towels, and curtains might brighten the home. The clothing of the peasant family again depended on the prosperity of the region and the family circumstances. It could range from the most simple and basic covering to elaborate and beautiful folk costumes" (Jelavich).

Although living conditions widely differed, they were nevertheless a far cry from modern houses with all amenities which the modern man enjoys. But in spite of this, there are authors who claim that the requirements of landowners were highly exaggerated. Josef Koetschet points out that the majority of the peasants maintained good relationships with the landowners who looked after them, offering help when the harvest was bad. This does not exclude some bad examples of cruel agas and beys, who used their private armies to extract as high agricultural surplus from their peasants.

Although the relationship between the peasant and the landlord was not ideal, the main problem was the rapacious and heavy-handed tax collectors. Majority of them were Muslims, some were Christians. The most odious practice they applied was to estimate taxes before the harvest. Apparently, the weakening central authority was not able to control them in the remote province of the empire such as Bosnia (Malcolm).

ECONOMY

Agriculture

Although Bosnia was more urbanized than Serbia and Bulgaria, still more than 80% of its population lived in villages. This determined a socio-economic structure in agriculture and played a pivotal role in the creation of GDP and provision of employment. Bosnian agriculture faced two obstacles in efforts to increase production and efficiency. One was objective, the other one was subjective. The objective obstacle stemmed from the size and distribution of the arable land. The subjective obstacle was caused by legal problems in regulating relationship between landowners and peasants.

1. Objective obstacles to increase in production and efficiency in agriculture

Bosnia has an unfavorable structure of agricultural land. More than half of the Bosnian soil was covered with forests. In addition, a great number of farms are located in hills and crass areas, where conditions for use of fertilizers were poor. Farms are of a small size, and a lot of labor input is needed to produce any crops. Land in the hills is sandy and rain washes it out, making the land infertile.

One quarter of the land in Bosnia was covered with meadows, pastures and unproductive soil. This means that only one quarter of the land was ready for productive use in raising crops.

The following table shows a structure of agricultural land in Bosnia in 1886.

Table 1 – Structure of agricultural land in Bosnia and Herzegovina
The whole area of Bosnia and Herzegovina 51,027 km²

Arable land	Gardens	Meadows	Vineyards	Forests	Pastures	Unproductive soil
11,032 km²	483 km²	3,465 km²	59 km²	26,581 km²	8,418 km²	989 km²
21,62%	0,95%	6,79%	0,11%	52,10%	16,50%	1,93%

SOURCE: KEMAL HRELJA: "Industrija Bosne I Hercegovine do kraja prvog svjetskog rata", (Industry of Bosnia and Herzegovina until the end of the WWI), Beograd 1961, p6

2. Subjective obstacles to increase in production and efficiency in agriculture

There were four characteristic types of relationships in agriculture. The first were free peasants, mostly Muslims, who had their own small *ciftliks*. As all other landowners they paid one tenth of the crop to the state. They tilled the soil themselves or with the help of the members of their families. Sometimes they would hire agricultural workers to do the job. Bigger landowners had workers, who farmed the land. They would pay between one quarter and one third of the crop to the landowner after deduction of the one tenth. This group consisted of relatively wealthy peasants who had their own animals for towing and used their own seed. They made up about 40% of all peasants. The third group were sharecroppers, who used the landowners' equipment, animals and seed, and who would retain about the half of the crop after paying one tenth to the state. The fourth group was in a most unfavorable position. Aside from paying all dues, they had to spend some time working for the landowner without being paid (corvee). Tahir Pasha's reform in 1848 abolished corvee and fixed the peasants dues at between one quarter and one third of the crop after deduction of one tenth. The landowners regarded this measure as an attack on their finances and tried to use extralegal methods to retain corvee.

After the reform, the peasant's burden was still great. The peasant could reckon to retain slightly more than one third of the crop. In order to tackle this burden, the peasant had to hire bigger portions of land, usually 20 hectares per family, compared to 3-4 hectares in Serbia. Institutional arrangements caused apathy among peasants, who did not have any impetus to increase production. The system in fact imposed progressive taxation, in which landowners and the state appropriated more than a half of the marginal product. In terminology of modern economic theory, Adam Smith's principles of taxation were not respected. Since the landowner could not force the tenant to invest more labor input, the tenant preferred free time to productive work. In addition, the landowner did not have any incentive to invest in agriculture, since a fall in rents and inflation demotivated them to intensify production. As a result, according to some estimates, agricultural productivity in Bosnia was between 1/3 and 2/5 of agricultural productivity in Bulgaria (Palairet).

The most fertile land was located in northern Bosnia. In the last years of the Ottoman rule, agricultural surpluses were exported to Dalmatia and Central Europe. Until 1864, the surplus amounted to 44% of total exports. The main exporting staple was wheat. This made northern towns in Bosnia lively trading centers until 1878. Northern Bosnia also exported plums via river harbor of Brcko on the river Sava, which accounted for almost one fifth of the total exports in 1858. Herzegovina was famous for its tobacco, which was also an important exporting item (Palairet).

Bosnia had better conditions for cattle-breeding, which was the most important industry after agriculture. Abundance of pastures and forests, alongside the fact that the peasant did not pay one tenth and one third for agricultural animals, created favorable conditions for cattle-breeding, which was a very developed industry. The strength of Bosnian cattle breeding lay in high quality and good racial features, rather than in its quantity. With slightly more than one million inhabitants, Bosnia was one of the richest countries in Europe measured by the number of cattle per person (Hrelja).

Small Industry

Small industry was the second most important economic activity. It shows a wide range of forms, from simple ones to very sophisticated ones. There were two types of small industry; homespun small industry and the town's small industry, imported from the East.

The first type of small industry was organized in cooperatives, closed organizations, typical for South Slav communities. These organizations made decorated and highly artistic products, which were consumed internally in a subsistence economy. In some villages production was expanded outside of cooperatives with a view of selling products in many markets in Bosnia, Serbia, Montenegro, Albania and the other parts of the Ottoman empire. (Hrelja)

An important group consisted of travelling artisans. Blacksmiths, horse-shoers, carpenters and construction workers offered their services in towns and villages. In return for their services, they received food, accommodation and clothes. They would sometimes get money for bigger services (Hrelja).

Town dwellers, on the other side, relied on services of the town artisans. Few artisan centers such as Sarajevo, Mostar, Travnik, Foca, Visoko, Tuzla and Bihac, were oases of small industries in the subsistence economy. In these towns trade of artisan products was organized in closed markets, called *bezistans*. Various products such as coarse fabric, wax, blankets, hide, furs and silk, were brought to these markets from all parts of the country and as far as Venice.

Artisans and merchants were organized in guilds. Members of the guild belonged to the same or similar profession. So, there were guilds of carpenters, stone-cutters, construction workers etc. Guilds were very powerful organizations. However, their strength weakened and they died out by the end of the Ottoman rule (Hrelja).

Mining

Mining had a long tradition in Bosnia. It dates back to the thirteen and fourteen centuries when it was promoted by German immigrants. Inertia of Turkish administration contributed to a decline in the mining industry, which was limited to a several mines such as Kresevo, Fojnica, Stari Majdan and Vares, where primitive methods in casting iron were used. In addition, there was a salt mine in Tuzla where salted wells provided material from which salt was extracted by boiling.

A new law was passed in 1869 with a view of modernizing the mining industry. The law divided minerals in several groups, set regulations regarding building the pits, regulated concessions and rules related to the mining police. The law enabled mine owners to research and exploit the land in search of ores without the state permission. The same law imposed something which could be called "health and safety regulations" in modern terminology. The owners and concessionaries were obliged to employ a doctor and pharmacist in mines and to compensate families of miners who died in accidents. Also, fines were imposed for those who violated miners' security.

Attempts to explore ores deposits and exploit it on a large scale did not produce any results. The main problem in implementation of the law was lying down in its collision with the understanding and adopted practice of the Ottoman property and real estate law. This law came into existence when there were not material grounds for its implementation in Bosnia (Schmid).

Forestry

The Balkans is a Turkish word, meaning mountains covered with forests. As a typical Balkan country Bosnia had a plenty of forests, which covered more than half of its territory. Therefore, forests represented a huge potential capital and a source of wealth and citizens' welfare. However, forestry was completely neglected under the Ottoman rule.

In the absence of organized exploitation of forest complexes, people relentlessly destroyed forests by clearing and burning woods with the aim of increasing the arable land. There was an attempt to regulate exploitation of forests by the Ottoman forests law, introduced in 1869. The law distinguished between four different types of ownership on forests; state, *vakuf,* municipal and private. A novelty was introduction of the state ownership and a clear definition what it meant. According to this law the peasants were allowed to use fuels and construction material for free in the state forests.

In spite of these attempts to modernize forestry in legal terms, their loose implementation did not contribute to any improvements. In the absence of a suitable state organization, capital, communications and infrastructure in general, forests remained a dead capital (Schmid).

Trade, Banking and Transport

In a predominantly subsistence economy, the use of money was limited. The peasant received money twice a year; once after the harvest, when he sold his products in the market, and second time when he was selling cattle. However, he would usually use the money obtained to settle previous debts. Most of needs the peasant produced himself together with members of his family; food, utensils, tools, clothes etc. It there was a trade between the peasants it usually took the form of a barter.

Foreign trade was much more developed than internal trade. Two historic events contributed to this; the Serbian uprising and Napoleonic continental blockade. Both these events diverted trading routes to the European Turkey. As a result, lucrative trade in colonial goods and cotton thrived. In addition, export of domestic products increased. The main exporting goods were wheat, tobacco, wine, fur, hides, plums, grapes, wood, iron, and some artisan products. The main importing items were coffee, sugar, tea, textile, weapons and luxury products. According to the report of the Italian consul, Bosnia recorded a surplus in trade balance in 1865 (Hrelja).

Low levels of internal trade created only rudimentary forms of money and credit. A small amount of gold money was in circulation. Its nominal value was backed by its content. However, many wars and turbulences prompted merchants to withdraw gold from circulation and to use it as a store of value. In 1876 the Ottoman bank issued banknotes worth 30 million paper grosz called "*kaimi*". These money was rapidly losing value, due to many unrests, so that confidence in it was shaken to the extent that merchants refused to accept it, prompting the Ottoman government to introduce severe fines for merchants. The loss of value of the paper money caused a sharp rise in prices.

There were several types of credit. The most successful one was agricultural credit, which was legally regulated by a Decree on establishment of credit institutions in agriculture, so called *menafi-sanduka*. This decree was enacted after the Crimean war. In a period 1867-1870 small credit institutions were created in 18 districts. Their task was to help the population in difficult times. The population of one district would bring a share of their crops, sell them, and put the money into the fund. They would receive 12% interest on their deposit.

Although Islam and Christianity explicitly forbid usury, it was widespread in some parts of the country. Loan sharks would charge exorbitant interest rates of 10% per week, which would amount to about 9,000% per annum, while official interest rate according to the Shariah law was 12% (*ribah*, which means yield in Arabic).

There was much more humane type of credit, friendly and individual. Wealthy individuals would give credits to friends, relatives and their apprentices without any guarantees. The only condition was that this transaction had to be kept in secrecy.

Commodity credits and mortgages were very limited and in a rudimentary form. Primitive forms of credit reflected the backwardness and subsistence economy in Bosnia before the Austro-Hungarian occupation (Hrelja).

The transport network reflected the backwardness of the country. Military roads built by the Romans were neglected, so the transport was even worse than in the medieval period. There were about 900 KM of carriage road, but the main transport means was a loaded horse. A great French geographer Ami Boue' made a classification of the Balkan roads, claiming that the lowest category in Bosnia and Albania was horrendous. He called these roads "*escaliers de rochers*", stairs of rocks (Malcolm).

Topal Osman-Pasha

Predominantly subsistence economy, a narrow internal market, backward transport network and primitive monetary and banking system were serious impediments to development of big industry in Bosnia. There were only several examples of successful big companies. In 1830s production of wooden planks started. They were exported, particularly to wine areas in France, where they got a reputation as "*murrain de Bosnie*". Inspite of simple tools, which were used in manufacturing of iron ore in Vares, the company was very profitable. This was due to workers' proficiency, which was recognized throughout the Balkans. (Domljan)

Around 1860 several rich merchants in Sarajevo established a limited company for producing coarse fabric. They invested capital of half a million of groats, which was a great sum of money at the time. Demand for coarse fabric was rising in a period of 7-8 years, which induced a rise in profit and share prices.

In 1876 Josip Feldbauer, merchant from Nova Gradiska, opened a beer factory in Sarajevo. The factory was taken over by a domestic merchant Risto Radul, but it was very soon closed down.

Two tobacco factories were opened with active government support. Monopoly on tobacco was introduced in 1875. Special concession was given to two domestic entrepreneurs, Kosta Skaric and Jovan Sterije Serezlija. They got permission to cut and prepare tobacco and to sell it in their own shops (Hrelja).

The penultimate decade of the Ottoman rule could be dubbed "the Golden Age of Bosnia". The driving force of modernization breakthrough was the benevolent and charismatic, the last Grand Vizier of Bosnia, Topal Osman Sherif Pasha. An excellent connoisseur of Arabic, Persian and Turkish literature, and a speaker of French and Greek, he was determined to improve lives of all Bosnians.

Topal Osman-Pasha was well acquainted with the situation in Bosnia. This enabled him to pacify unrest on the border with Montenegro and the Austro-Hungary and to carry out reforms. He expanded foreign trade by sending merchants to Western Europe. He opened many schools for Muslims, a big library at the Bey Mosque, and encouraged Christians to expand the network of their schools (Younis).

A railway was built, connecting Banjaluka with a Croatian border. The following roads were built: Sarajevo-Bosanski Brod, Sarajevo-Mostar, Sarajevo-Visegrad-Novi Pazar, Maglaj-Donja Tuzla, Donja Tuzla-Brcko-Bijeljina-Zvornik, via

MajevicaBosanska Gradiska-Banjaluka, Travnik-Livno, and Trebinje-Dubrovnik (Koetschet).

The greatest beneficiary of Topal Osman-Pasha's reform was Sarajevo, which became the cultural and intellectual center of the country. The Vilayet constitution in 1865 envisaged the opening of printing houses. A printing house opened in Sarajevo was accompanied by publication of several newspapers. A telegraph was opened connecting Sarajevo to Istanbul, via Novi Pazar. A new electric sowing machine came to Sarajevo. Two hospitals, one civil, and one military, were opened in Sarajevo, providing free health care to citizens. A new, modern pharmacy, was opened, replacing home made herbs and balms with Western medicine. It had a pharmacist and an assistant. A photographer shop and a dry-cleaning shop appeared in Sarajevo. New winds were blowing in Sarajevo, bringing *alla-franca* (modern) life style, and blending it with *alla- turca,* (traditional) life style (Younis).

In-spite of these improvements the situation in Bosnia was not good, with some claiming that life had been better forty years ago. (Malcolm) The main problem in Bosnia was the heavy burden on the peasants and unresolved agrarian relationships. Two uprisings broke, one in Herzegovina, and one in Bosanska Krajina in a period 1875-78. Even before, many unrests, and harsh reprisals by the authorities, prompted thousands of peasants to flee to Austro-Hungary. The Austro-Hungarian government spent six million crowns only in one year to support the refugees. A weak central government in Istanbul was not able to control its most North-Western province anymore. This is why the big powers decided in the Congress of Berlin that Austro-Hungary should occupy Bosnia and put it under its administration (Schmid).

CHAPTER TWO

AUSTRO-HUNGARIAN INTEREST IN BOSNIA AND HERZEGOVINA

The interest of Austria-Hungary, or its constituent countries, Austria and Hungary, dates back to the Middle Ages. It had developed and changed under the influence of historical, internal, and external factors.

HISTORICAL BACKGROUND

Bosnia was mentioned for the first time in the geographic-political manuscript of the Byzantian emperor Constantin Porfirogenet in 1058, as a separate territory around the river Bosnia, which belongs to the Serbs. Parts of modern Bosnia and Herzegovina were ruled by the Croatian governor for several decades in the eleventh century.

After death of the Serbian ruler Bodin in 1101, the focus of Serbian political activities moved to the east, where *Rascia* was established, as a core of the Serbian medieval state. At the same time Croatia entered into a personal union with Hungary, when in 1102, with the act called *Pacta Conventa*, the Hungarian king Koloman became the Croatian king. Bosnia fell under the Hungarian influence, although it had its own ruler, the ban, who was a good deal independent of the Hungarian influence, using the remoteness of his country.

In the 1160s and 1170s, Croatia and Bosnia fell under the Byzantium rule after successful expansionist military expedition of its emperor Manuel Komnen. However, after his death Bosnia managed to escape the Byzantian grip, and at the same time wriggled out of the Hungarian control, becoming for the first time an independent state. (Malcolm)

In-spite of this the Hungarian-Croatian kingdom remained the main threat to Bosnian independence. Hungarian kings had tried to subject Bosnia to its rule, considering Bosnia the underbelly of its state. In order to achieve this, Hungarian kings exercised a strong political and military pressure on Bosnia, with a view of subduing it. In the fourth decade of the twelfth century Hungarian kings considered themselves as the rulers of Bosnia. In one of the charters of the Hungarian king Bela in 1137, Bosnia was mentioned as *Bosniensis ducatus*, one of the dukedoms in his kingdom.

Links between Hungary and Bosnia, were not, however, one-sided. The first Bosnian duke, Boric ban, actively participated in Hungarian affairs. In the Hungarian Byzantium war, he joined Hungarian troops with his detachments during the siege of Branicevo, the village in modern-day north-east Serbia.

Boric Ban was also actively involved in a dynastic struggle for the Hungarian throne. The winner, Istvan (Stephan) IV, rewarded him for his support with large swathes of land in Slavonia in 1168, where he fled after Manuel Komnen temporarily overrun Bosnia in his 1166/67 military campaign (Imamovic).

After gaining independence, Bosnia's ruler Kulin Ban was welcoming *patarens* and *catarrhs*, heretics who were persecuted and expelled from Italy and France. The Serbian duke Vukan warned the Pope Innocent III in 1199 about the spread of heresy in Bosnia. He turned to the Hungarian king Emerik, asking him to intervene and undertake all necessary activities to nip the heresy in a bud. Emerik immediately accepted the invitation of the Pope, hoping that he might achieve his political goals in Bosnia with the aid of the Rome. (Imamovic). Kulin Ban shrewdly pretended that he did not know the difference between Catholicism and heresy and asked the Pope to send

Catholic priests to Bosnia to educate the masses. Unlike other countries, "heresy" in Bosnia was accepted not only by poor masses, but also by powerful nobility. Nevertheless, Kulin ban did not want war with Hungary and the Rome, and at the meeting at Bilino Polje in 1203 promised to return the country to the "real faith" (Mahmutefendic).

In a period of more than two centuries after gaining independence Bosnia had three strong rulers; Kulin Ban (1180-1204), Stjepan Kotromanic (1322-1353) and Tvrtko (1353-1391). During their reign Bosnia increased in size, acquiring Hum (Herzegovina), and great parts of nowadays Serbia and Dalmatia. King Tvrtko was coronated in 1377 as a king of Bosnia, Serbia, Dalmatia, and the Coastal area. During this period Hungary was the most powerful neighboring country. Serbia expanded significantly and became the empire. However, it had not had ambitions to conquer Bosnia. Hungarian rulers were dissuaded by the fact that Bosnia was pretty un-accessible land, and that even when conquered, invaders would face unruly and rebellious domestic nobility (Malcolm).

In such a situation Hungary wanted to use the church policy to exercise its control over Bosnia, rather than to wage a war. Bosnia, which was predominantly a Catholic country, (unlike Herzegovina, which was mainly Christian Orthodox), was in religious matters part of a Dubrovnik diocese. The church hierarchy in Dubrovnik did not interfere much in religious affairs in Bosnia, due to a great distance, and allowed the Catholic Church in Bosnia to appoint its own bishops. Hungary wanted to establish a tighter control over Bosnian religious affairs. In order to achieve this, Hungary wanted to put Bosnia's Catholic Church under the jurisdiction of the archbishop in Split, who was pro-Hungarian.

In the next half century, Bosnia was under constant pressure from its powerful neighbor, Hungary. Hungarians did not give up on their attempts to gain control over Bosnia's diocese. In the 1230s, popes required from Hungarian rulers and bishops to eradicate the heresy in Bosnia. This was partially a reaction to the low level of education of Bosnian clergy, many of them illiterate, and not acquainted with the ritual of baptism. Using this as an excuse, Hungary raided Bosnia in 1238, conquering the southern and the eastern parts of the country, and trying to introduce the Dominican church order. However, faced with the Mongol threat in 1241, Hungarians had to withdraw from Bosnia, being significantly weakened with heavy military defeat and devastation of their country (Malcolm).

Mongols circumvented Bosnia in their onslaught, which enabled the Bosnian ruler, Ban Ninoslav Matej, to consolidate his power. The Ban felt so powerful that he accepted the invitation of the citizens of Split, who were on a war foot with the king Bela IV, to help them in the war they waged with the town of Trogir in 1243/44, which was loyal to the Hungarian king (Imamovic).

Ban Matej Ninoslav was mentioned for the last time in 1249, when he renewed the agreement with Dubrovnik. After the seat of the Bosnian diocese was moved to Djakovo in Croatia, under the jurisdiction of the Hungarian archbishop Kaloci, Bela IV started the war against Bosnia in 1253, in which he managed to crash the resistance. Ninoslav's cousin and heir, Prijezda sided with the Hungarians. As a reward he got the county Novake in Slavonia. The Bosnian state was divided. Prijezda ruled in Bosnia proper and the lower bordering area, while Usora and Soli were given to the Serbian king Stefan Dragutin, who was a Hungarian vassal (Imamovic). The northeastern part was joined with a territory in northern Serbia to form a Hungarian dukedom called Macva (Malcolm).

Bosnia increased its territory considerably under its second powerful ruler Stjepan Kotromanic. After defeating the Bosnian ruler for the first two decades of the fourteenth century, Subic ban, he expanded the Bosnian territory to the west, acquiring land which previously belonged to Croatia. After that he conquered two hundred miles of the Dalmatian coast between

Dubrovnik and Split. In 1326 he annexed the greatest part of Hum (Herzegovina), creating for the first time Bosnia and Herzegovina as one political unit. Until then, Hum was a fairly independent entity under the rule of the local nobility, and religiously separate from Bosnia since the majority of population were Christian Orthodox (Malcolm).

When Stjepan Kotromanic died he left the Bosnian state independent, affluent, and powerful. However, its stability depended on the co-operation of the powerful nobility, who had strongholds in various parts of the country. Stjepan Kotromanic's nephew Tvrtko was only 15 years old when he inherited the throne. He had neither the authority nor military strength to control the centrifugal forces in his country. A Hungarian king again grabbed the opportunity to acquire some territory in Bosnia. In the first fourteen years of kingship, he had to tackle rebellions in his country and Hungarian pretensions. In 1366 he even had to plead for Hungarian help after his enemies wanted to bring to the throne his rival and brother Vuk. But already in 1367 Tvrtko was again at the throne. Hungarians, busy with problems at its northern border, left Tvrtko on his own (Malcolm).

A Hungarian king renewed his interest for Bosnia towards the end of the fourteenth century, despite a heavy defeat against the Ottoman troops in 1396. In 1404 Hungary was again involved in Bosnian dynastic strives, when the nobility expelled king Ostoja from the country and replaced him with illegitimate Tvrtko's son Tvrtko II. Ostoja returned to Bosnia with a Hungarian army and regained a part of the country. With Hungarian help, he returned to the throne within ten years and helped in mending the relationship between them and Hrvoje Vukcic Hrvatinic, the most powerful Bosnian nobleman (Malcolm).

Hungary did not give up on Bosnia even after the Ottomans conquered it in 1463. The Hungarian king Mathias Corvinus run over the northern and the northwestern part of Bosnia. He established two counties, the Jajce county, and the Srebrenica county where he built a ring of fortresses which will later evolve into a military border. (*Militar Grenze*). He had great plans to restore the Bosnian kingdom in a limited form. In order to achieve this he appointed a great nobleman Nicola from Ilok a new Bosnian king (1471-1477). However, this did not have any link with an independent Bosnian state, but was more the result of his internal aims and Hungarian interests.

The Hungarian system of defense was, however, exposed to more intensive Turkish onslaughts from the southeast. The system was constantly undermined resulting in Turkish conquest of the Srebrenica county in 1519-20, and the Jajce county in 1527-28 (Bronza).

A decisive event occurred in 1526. At the battle of Mohac the Ottomans delivered Hungarians a crushing defeat. Turks subsequently conquered Hungary, and ruled the Hungarian-Croatian kingdom for more than a century and a half. This gave the Habsburgs an opportunity to revive the ideological concept of the inheritance of the Hungarian rulers and claimed their irrevocable right on Bosnia (Bronza).

THE EASTERN QUESTION

Austro-Hungarian foreign policy, and its attitude to the Eastern question, as part of it, was shaped by a combination of internal and external factors.

1. Internal factors
a) In the seventeenth and eighteenth century Austria was a huge empire, a conglomerate of political and legal arrangements and a mosaic of different ethnic groups, nations, regions and states. It stretched from Galicia in the east to Switzerland in the west. Its territory had 700,000 square kilometers, comprising the area of nowadays Austria, Hungary, the Czech Republic, the Slovak Republic, Belgium, Luxembourg, and parts of

Italy, Poland, Ukraine, Romania, Croatia, and Serbia (Bronza), and consisted of eleven nationalities; Germans, Hungarians, Czechs, Slovaks, Croats, Serbs, Slovenes, Italians, Rumanians, Poles, and Little Russians (Gross). It looked with one eye to the west, to the German lands, The Roman empire, the Spanish succession in the Latin America, and with the other eye to the Balkans and Eastern Europe. At a certain point it had possessions in the Atlantic, and Madras in India. Such a political power and even greater political and military ambitions were not matched with economic strength. Compared to Western Europe it had a petrified institutional and administrative structure, ossified feudal structure, and outdated economic structure. The latter was a particularly strong impediment to modern economic growth.

Although the empire was a customs union externally, it had been fragmented with smaller customs unions within. Most internal tariffs in the Austrian half of the monarchy were abolished only in 1775, in the Hungarian part in 1784, and the ones between the two halves of the monarchy were removed only in 1851 (Gross). The economy of the Monarchy was even more hindered with an extreme version of mercantilist economic policy. It consisted of very restrictive import quotas and outright imports prohibitions; high duties on the permitted imports, as well as high taxes or even prohibitions on many primary export commodities. Exports were encouraged, including some primary products such as Galician grain, of which surplus supplies were considered available. This foreign trade system was accompanied by various aspects of Habsburg mercantilism, such as the ban on emigration and the encouragement of certain types of immigrants, with a view of increasing population, and subsequent supply of workforce and a fall in wages. Habsburg autarchy was partly caused by underdeveloped commercial sector and poor transport links with Western Europe. In addition, most Habsburg possessions were not advantageously situated within the network of world trade. If wholesale and foreign trade was crucial for the accumulation of capital and development of entrepreneurship, its small extent in the Austrian economy was particularly damaging to the modern capitalist development, when foreign trade, especially with the North and South America, played such a decisive role in stimulating industrial and agricultural production (Gross).

As a result, the main concern of the Austrian version of mercantilism was not the balance of payments, but unbalanced internal regional development, in which eastern provinces became "periphery", supplying low-cost foodstuffs and raw materials to the western industrialized regions, and market for high-valued industrial products coming from the "core". Retarded economic growth compared to western Europe, and frequent wars put a permanent strain on the government budget, resulting in constant deficits, and prompting the issue of paper-money, the *Bankozettel*. (Gross)

b) The outdated institutional structure was also an impediment to economic development and further territorial expansion. The forces of modern transformation, which were plentiful in Britain and some other western European countries, were lacking in Austria. Vested interest of ruling classes obstructed mobility and impeded innovation, petrifying institutional structure which was inimical to rationalization, to secularization, and the primacy of material progress. Among historical factors which contributed to retardation of development many scholars ascribe importance to the damage caused by the Counter-Reformation (Gross).

In addition, the "emancipation" decrees of Joseph II, whose aim was to grant personal freedom to all remaining serfs, was limited to the Crown lands, while eastern provinces were bogged down in ossified feudalism (Gross). In addition, Austrian emperors believed in the divine nature of their ruling position (*Gottesgnadentum*) rather than the one which will rely on the strength of the army. As Eugen de Savoy pointed out, the security of the "Pragmatic Sanction" could have been better achieved with sound finances and the strong army of 180,000 soldiers rather than with formal signature of some useless papers. In 1737 Austria had 275 marshals and generals, but none of them had the necessary expertise and experience (Bronza).

c) The lack of consistency of the Austrian treatment of the Eastern Question could be partially ascribed to different attitudes of its rulers. Leading figures at the court as well as high brass were involved in mutual conflicts. As a result, Austrian politics was depraved of any integrity. Maria Tereza was against an alliance with Russia and against the war against Turkey. She was not in favor of the division of the Ottoman empire, claiming that Austria would get nothing except deserted, worthless territories inhabited by unreliable Greeks even if it expanded to Constantinople. Her friendly inclination to the Ottoman Empire remained in place for more than 40 years of her rule. She wanted to extend this friendship by promoting Turkish culture in Austria through adoption of Turkish fashion (*Turqerie*) and massive incorporation of the Ottoman iconography and Turkish way of dressing. (Bronza). On the other hand, her son Joseph II established close relationships with Catholics in Bosnia, and wanted to liberate the Balkan Christians from the Turkish yoke. In that respect he was in favor of military alliance with Russia and the war against Turkey, whose aim would be a dissolution of the Ottoman Empire, and annexation of its parts, including Bosnia and Herzegovina, to Austria. He was supported by his diplomats Kaunitz and Kobelenz (Bronza).

2. External factors

    After the Hungarian troops were defeated at the battle of Mohac in 1526, the Habsburgs used the political vacuum, namely the dying out of the Jagiellonian dynasty, to acquire the territory of the Hungarian kingdom, when the Austrian archduke Ferdinand was coronated as the king of Hungary in 1527. With this act the Habsburgs incorporated all the Hungarian traditions, including the centuries long tradition of the Hungarian kings to consider themselves the kings of Bosnia.

The Eastern question was dormant for a century and a half, waiting for an Austrian counteroffensive against the Ottoman troops. This occurred at the end of the seventeenth century when the Austrian army heavily defeated the Ottoman army in the Viennese war. The Habsburg treatment of Bosnia and Herzegovina was a special chapter in the history of the Viennese war. Austria got the opportunity to reactivate a historical concept of the Hungarian rulers' heritage to claim an inalienable right to Bosnia and Herzegovina. This stance was also supported by church dignitaries. When Venice tried to penetrate the territory of Bosnia and Herzegovina from the south the Austrians prevented them by exercising political pressure, emphasizing its political right to Bosnia which belonged to the Hungarian kings (Bronza).

A strength of the Austrian empire has significantly increased in the first couple of decades of the XVIII century. Around 1720 it surpassed France in international arena of the great powers, while Spain became a second rank power. After another victory against the Ottoman empire in the 1716-1718 war the Austrian empire had an upper hand in the area south and north of the river Danube. After the Pozarevac peace in 1718 the Ottoman empire had to relinquish the norther parts of Serbia and Bosnia to Austria. At that time, the Ottoman empire did not pose any threat to the Austrian empire. Austria became the most important international power in the context of the resolution of the Eastern Question (Bronza).

Things turned to the worst to the Austrian empire after its defeat against the Ottoman empire in the 1737-1739 war. The peace of Sremski Karlovci in 1739 returned to the Ottoman empire all the territories south of the rivers Sava and Danube. In addition, the wars waged in the Central and Western Europe from 1740 until 1763 further diluted Austrian military strength and the ability to exert political and military influence in the Balkans. Its activities in Bosnia and Herzegovina until the end of the eighteenth century were mainly confined to inefficient espionage and contacts with Franciscan priests (Bronza).

During the eighteenth century, Bosnia and Herzegovina was never on the top of the list of the Austrian priorities in foreign policy. The Austrian empire looked at more lucrative opportunities in Germany and Italy. In addition, it had great ambitions in competition with the Great Britain, France, the Netherlands, and Prussia in quest for world supremacy. However, the Austrian empire overestimated its capability. It lagged behind the afore-mentioned countries economically. Also, those countries were already well- established nation states, while Austrian lacked national homogeneity and was corroded by its many nations' struggle for emancipation and better position within the empire.

All weaknesses of the Austrian empire were reflected in its policy related to the Eastern Question. This policy lacked aims and strategic coherence. It was rough, unsophisticated and relied on a brute force and aggression. As a result, Austria underestimated the Ottoman empire, its main opponent in the Balkans, and failed to capitalize on victories in the two wars.

Even in its Balkan policy, Bosnia was not a first priority. Austria was more interested in Serbia, and access to the Morava valley, Danube, and the Black Sea. Austria tried to mobilize the Christian population in the Balkans to fight the Ottomans, playing on its subjection on a religious basis. However, having a deeply religious approach, Austria did not convince Christian Orthodox population that in the case of its takeover of Bosnia and Herzegovina Muslim oppression would not be replaced by the same or even worse Catholic oppression (Bronza).

It required eighteen century and the German unification for Austria to pay more attention to Bosnia and Herzegovina.

AUSTRIA, THE GERMAN UNIFICATION, AND BOSNIA AND HERZEGOVINA

Germany was devastated after the Thirty-Year War. It felt negative consequences of the war for two centuries. A French diplomat stated that the Treaty of Westfalia was "the finest jewel in the King of France's crown, because it had kept Germany disunited" (Enderink). At the end of the eighteen century, Germany was divided into 300 independent states. Each and every of them had its owner ruler, government, monetary and fiscal policy and levied customs on imports from other countries. Such a state of affairs was a gross impediment to economic and political development (Mahmutefendic).

Ironically, it was Napoleon who paved a way for the unification of Germany. His military victories at Austerlitz in 1805, and Jena in 1806, led to a dissolution of the Holy Roman Empire in 1806 and merge of some German states, whose number was reduced to 39.

First attempts for partial political unification were undertaken in 1806 by the establishment of the Rhineland confederation. This was followed by a confederation in 1815. The German Confederation (*Deutsche Bund)* was created by the Concert of Europe, with a task assigned to Austria to lead the German states in creating a buffer between France and Russia that would ensure European stability (Enderink).

In monetary affairs German states were in disarray. At the beginning of XIX century there were 70 currencies only in Rhineland. First attempts to reduce the number of currencies in circulation and put monetary affairs in order were undertaken in 1837 by the establishment of *Munzverein* (coinage union). A group of southern states entered in a treaty in Munich in 1837, based on 24.5 gulden (or florin) to the Cologne mark (3608 English grains or 233.85 metric grains of fine silver). In 1838 a group of northern states adopted the Prussian thaler standard, defined as 14 to the Cologne mark. The Dresden convention fixed the exchange rate at 4 Prussian thalers to 7 gulden. This reduced the number of coinages from previous seven to two. The silver standard was adopted with the exception of a free city of Bremen whose monetary system rested on a gold basis.

Austria did not join the union since it had a long history of inconvertible paper money. The regulation of paper money in circulation remained unresolved.

A new *Munzverein* was established in 1857 by Vienna Convention after a year of negotiation. The agreement abandoned the Cologne mark of silver for a *Zollpfund* (customs-union pound) of 500 grams, divided metrically. Thirty thalers, 52.5 south German florins and 45 Austrian florins were to be coined from a *Zollpfund* of silver. This produced a simplified exchange rate structure of 1 thaler =1.75 south German florins =1.5 Austrian florins. A new gold coin crown was to be minted and used only in international transactions. As part of the agreement Austria returned to banknote convertibility into silver in September 1858 (Mahmutefendic).

While Austria managed to get involved in a gradual move towards monetary unification of the German states it failed to join the Customs Union (*Zollverein*), which was created in 1834.

Before the Napoleonic wars, the hundreds of small German states set barriers to mutual trade. In addition, each state also had numerous internal barriers such as local and regional tithes, tolls, taxes, internal tariffs etc. The Prussian reformers of 1807 attempted to address the issues of "customs regulations and toll and excise revenues and to create a Prussian tariff-free zone. Manufacturing groups put the pressure on the Prussian government to remove internal tariffs, but also called for the economy to be protected from exports from France and Great Britain (Endernik). This was in accordance with a teaching of the great Prussian economist Friedrich List, who advocated free internal trade within the German states and protectionist international trade (Brue & Grant).

Between 1818, when Prussia abolished its internal tariffs, and 1834, when the *Zollverein* was established, three customs unions were in existence; In the south, Bavaria and Wurttemberg, in the north, Prussia, and Hessen-Darmstadt), and a third in the middle, comprising Hannover, Brunswick, Nassau, Hessen-Kassel, Frankfurt-am-Main, Saxony and the small Thuringian states). Prussia established control over the Southern and the Northern customs unions, but suspected Austrian involvement in the creation of the "Middle German Commercial Union". (Enderink)

The Middle German Commercial Union was a thorn in Prussia's eye, since Austria supported it as a wedge between the other two customs unions under Prussian control. However, Prussia managed to successfully encircle the middle union when it reached an agreement with the Netherlands about shipping on the Rhine in 1831, and connected its western and eastern provinces by accepting Hessen-Kassel into the northern union. This broke the backbone of the Middle German Commercial Union. The last attempt was made by Austria to obstruct the creation of the German customs union when together with Great Britain it enticed Hanover to start negotiations within the German Confederation, which were rebuffed by Prussia. One year later the southern union of Bavaria and Wurttemberg was absorbed into the northern *Zollverein*). (Enderink) (Henderson: "The Rise of German Industrial Power").

Austria did not join the German Zollverein. Powerful Prussian landowners (*junkers*) were against the removal of tariffs on imports of cheap agricultural products from eastern provinces of the Austrian empire. The same applies to Austrian manufacturing groups, who were threatened by the possibility of cheap exports of manufacturing products from Prussia and the other German states.

Austria unsuccessfully tried to obstruct the functioning of the German Zollverein in the 1850s and the first half of the 1860s. The problem for Austria was that it did not offer any attractive and viable alternative to the Zollverein to the other German states. Its mercantilist and protectionist policy were outdated and unattractive to modern industrial development.

But it was politics and national sentiments rather than disputes about tariff policy that shaped a direction of the German unification.[1] Although modern usage of the term nationalism has its origin in the American and French revolution, the term *Nationalismus* has a Prussian origin and dates back to the German romanticist Herder. Nationalism was widespread among artists and intellectuals in general, and was considered to have roots in German culture and language. The problem German nationalists faced was that the German Confederation contained areas in which majority of population were not German native speakers while there were regions outside the German Confederation in which German native-speakers made up majority.

There were three possible solutions of the German question. In the first one the German Confederation would join the German Austria, which would be carved out of the Austrian empire (*Grossdeutch Losung)-The Great Germany solution*. In the second one the German Confederation would join the Austrian empire. In the third one the German Confederation would create the new German state without Austria (*kleindeutsch Losung). The Small Germany Solution*. The first solution was unacceptable to the Habsburgs, who would not give up on their centuries long tradition of being an imperial power. The second solution was unacceptable to German nationalists who did not want any multiethnic, but national German state. Austria wanted a seventy-million multinational, cosmopolitan,

---

[1] The famous French philosopher Ernest Renan (1823-1892), well known for his cynical quip directed to those who claimed that humans' freedom was *ius naturalis*:" Yes, humans are born free, but they are also born naked. However, if they walk in a street naked in the most liberal country they will be arrested", noted in 1882: "Community of interest brings about trade agreements, but nationality has a sentimental side to it; it is both soul and body at once; a *Zollverein* is not a *patrie*. (Enderink)

Austrian-German led empire with Vienna as a capital. Prussia wanted the German national state with Berlin as its capital city.[2]

Military events, aided by demographic trends, shaped the direction of the German unification. The German Austrian population, in terms of percentage, was shrinking both within the German Confederation and within the Austrian empire itself. In the 1820s German Austrians accounted for 27% of the German Confederation and 37% of the Austrian Empire. By the 1860s it the German Austrians accounted for 24% of the population of the German Confederation and 34% of the Austrian Empire. In the same period, the percentage of Prussians within the German Confederation increased from 33% to 39%. (Breuilly, Austria, Prussia and Germany 1806-1871)

Austria was drawn into a battle at Solferino against Piedmont in 1859. What was expected to be a decisive victory turned into a catastrophic defeat when France joined the battle, resulting in the loss of Lombardy. Prussia failed to come to rescue. Austria and Prussia came together in the war with Denmark in 1864, when the two German states acted as allies in an attempt to prevent the integration of the majority German duchies of Schleswig-Holstein into a Danish state. While paying lip service to the alliance with Austria Bismarck nevertheless tried to obstruct Austrian policy concerning the two duchies (Okey, The Habsburg Monarchy c. 1765-1918).

A decisive event occurred in 1866 when Prussia defeated Austria in a battle at Sadova/Konigsgratz in Bohemia. This put the last nail in a coffin of any attempts to create a German state which would include Austria. A year later Hungary put a pressure on

---

[2] This difference is reflected in the two variants of the German language. Austrian German assimilated many words of non-German origin, which is a characteristic of all imperial languages. For example, apricot is *Apricose* in German variant of German, and *Marilene*, a word of Slavic origin, in Austrian German. Pancake is *Pfannekuche* in German variant of German and *Palacinke*, a word of Hungarian origin, in Austrian German. Unlike Austrians Germans insist on linguistic purity; they do not use international words radio and television, but *Funk* and *Fernsehen* respectively.

weakened Austria to reform the Empire. The result was *Ausgleich* (Compromise), which turned the Austrian Empire into a dual monarchy called Austro-Hungary, comprising two states integrated into a personal union embodied in a common emperor Franz Joseph, common army, and three common ministries; the ministry of war, the ministry of foreign affairs and the ministry of finance. Hungarians took over the ministry of foreign affairs, turning the interest of a dual monarchy towards Bosnia and Herzegovina. In a memorandum to the European great powers of 21st April 1878, the Austro-Hungarian foreign minister Gyula Andrassy made a case for the Habsburg occupation of Bosnia and Herzegovina. He pointed out that Bosnia and Herzegovina were not equipped for autonomous development. A great power was therefore needed to bring prosperity, the rule of law and above everything to carry out a cultural mission in the country which was as backward as some of European external colonies after more than four centuries of the Ottoman rule (Mahmutefendic).

Andrassy's idea was to leave Bosnia and Herzegovina formally a part of the Ottoman Empire for thirty years. Austria-Hungary would rule the two provinces until the Ottoman Empire reforms and modernizes itself. After thirty years Bosnia and Herzegovina would be returned to the Ottoman rule. In a meantime the only link with the Ottoman Empire would be maintained through the personality of the sultan Abdul Hamid. His pictures would be displayed in public places, his birthdays would be publicly celebrated, and his name would be mentioned in prayers in mosques.

The Congress of Berlin made decisions which were in line with Andrassy's proposals. However, Turkey did not modernize, and Bosnia and Herzegovina were not returned to the Ottoman rule. It was annexed by the Austro-Hungary in 1908 and remained its part until the dissolution of the Monarchy in 1918.

CHAPTER THREE

LITERATURE ON THE AUSTRO-HUNGARIAN PERIOD IN BOSNIA AND HERZEGOVINA

There is a voluminous literature which deals with the Austro-Hungarian period in Bosnia and Herzegovina. Many authors, domestic and foreign, historians, lawyers, political scientists, economists and physicians wrote either about certain aspect of this era, or analyzed the entire period. Most works were written by historians and economists. There is a significant overlap in their works. Historians could not avoid economic topics, while economists had to deal with historically relevant events.

For this purpose, authors are divided into four groups: 1. Domestic historians, 2. Foreign historians, 3. Domestic economists, and 4. Foreign economists.

1. Domestic historians

Hamdija Kapidzic did not pay much attention to economic achievements of the Austro-Hungary in Bosnia and Herzegovina. There is only one chapter dedicated to economic matters, in which he analyses in detail a sale of Steinbeis timber factory. Due to its enormous strategic importance to the Bosnian economy, the Land government did not want to sell the factory to an Italian businessman, but preferred nationalization, although it was struggling with the public finance. (Kapidzic).

In his assessment of the Austro-Hungarian rule in Bosnia and Herzegovina Kapidzic focused on three areas; 1. agriculture, 2. the electoral law, and 3. the political system.

1. Kapidzic emphasizes the fact that Austro-Hungary did not do anything to improve the position of the landless peasants. The old system of agricultural relationships was inherited from the Ottoman period, in which the peasants were burdened by one tenth of the harvest paid to the government, and one third of the remaining amount to the landlord. In addition, greedy and corrupt officials and tax collectors fleeced the peasant whenever they could. As a result, many of them emigrated either to Serbia or to the United States of America. Kallay tried to clamp down on corruption. Also, he suggested aid to the peasants in kind. However, his proposal was refused under the argument that the peasants' situation was not bad (Kapidzic).

2. Kapidzic is critical of the curial electoral system, which excluded many layers of population from voting. The system cemented religious and class division of the Bosnian society. It deliberately excluded the Social Democratic Party of Bosnia and Herzegovina from the Parliament, the only non-sectarian and non-nationalist political party, which could jeopardize *divide et impera* government policy (Kapidzic).

3. The Bosnian parliament (*Bosanski sabor*) had more competencies than the Croatian Parliament and provincial Diets and was in charge of more affairs than the former. However, it could not participate in the foreign policy. Also, all laws passed by the Parliament had to be approved firstly by the Austrian and the Hungarian Parliament, and secondly by the emperor Frantz Joseph. Kapidzic concludes that this was the best proof of the colonial status of Bosnia and Herzegovina. While this is partially true, one needs to bear in mind that the situation in the Austrian Parliament was not much better. Frantz Joseph ruled Austria proper by decree. He could have dissolved the Parliament and

abolished the laws passed in the Austrian Parliament as he wished (Duikers Jackson William J. & Spielvogel J). So, one could say that the limited powers of the Bosnian parliament were less the result of the colonial status of the country but owed more to a democratic deficit in Austria itself, whose march to democracy was shaky after experience of the Bach's absolutism.

Dzevad Juzbasic points out an absolutist character of the administration in Bosnia and Herzegovina. Occupied territories had neither their representatives, not their population was represented in the representative organs of the Austria-Hungary. The emperor was a carrier of the sovereignty of Bosnia and Herzegovina, and the carrier of legislative power before the provinces got a constitution in 1910. The only exception were economic and financial affairs in which the two parliaments, the Austrian and the Hungarian, were in charge. This status prompted some Austrian politicians, including Leo Bilinsky, the minister of finance who succeeded Istvan Burian, to describe a political status of Bosnia and Herzegovina resembling a colony (Juzbasic).

Juzbasic provides a detailed analysis of shared responsibilities of Austria and Hungary in mismanagement of the economic affairs of Bosnia and Herzegovina. The Austrian economy was much more compatible with the Bosnian economy. This is why the Austrians wanted a quick incorporation of Bosnia and Herzegovina into the Monarchy's customs union, while Hungarians were hesitant. In general, the Austrians espoused much friendly behavior to Bosnia and Herzegovina compared to the Hungarians. However, beneath this friendliness lied the interest of Austria to develop manufacturing industry in the country which will not compete with the Austrian manufacturing industry. While the Austrian manufacturing industry produced final goods of a high technological value the manufacturing industry of Bosnia and Herzegovina was dominated with a production of raw materials and semi-manufactured goods of low technological value. As a result, the Bosnian exports was three times imports in volume, but less in value.

In the first decade of the twentieth century exports of raw materials accounted for 83% of the total value of goods sold abroad. Final products accounted for two thirds of the value of imports. The main exporting staples were semi-processed wood, agricultural products, ores, pig iron, iron ware and chemical products. Textile and furniture were imported (Juzbasic).

The only exception was forestry industry, which managed to escape the colonial pattern. At the end of the nineteenth century a big forestry industry, which posed a threat to the Austrian forestry industry in the world market, was developed. Owing to privileges which the occupation government gave foreign private capital in terms of minimum payment of dues and discount on transport by railways, foreign owners managed to sell Bosnian lumber at the price which was 20-25 lower compared to the Austrian lumber. This caused consternation in the Austrian business circles who complained of "*Bosnische Gefahr*"- the Bosnian danger (Juzbasic).

According to Juzbasic Hungarian influence on the Bosnian economic affairs was much more detrimental compared to the Austrian influence. Apart from the attempts to reduce the competencies of the Bosnian

Parliament, damaging Hungarian influence was reflected in agriculture, heavy industry and transport.

Hungarians were against the solution of the agrarian problem, which was arguably the biggest cancer in the tissue of the Bosnian economy and society. Powerful Hungarian landowners were afraid that the agrarian reform in Bosnia and Herzegovina would be a "bad example", which would prompt the solution of the agrarian question in Hungary. In addition, Hungary tried to restrict competition of the Bosnian agricultural products fearing that it would harm Hungarian agriculture. The same applies to heavy industry, which was the most developed manufacturing industry in Hungary. However, unlike Bosnia and Herzegovina, Hungary did not have resources for development of a heavy industry and was aware of comparative advantages which the Bosnian heavy industry possessed.

All of this was possible because Hungary had a virtual monopoly in transportation policy. It was able to manipulate transport tariffs in its favor.

Juzbasic has an overall negative assessment of the transportation policy. Narrow-gauge railways prevailed in Bosnia and Herzegovina. They were a serious impediment to the economic development (Juzbasic).

Juzbasic did not analyze development of a road transport in Bosnia and Herzegovina. He did not provide data for manufacturing industry, agriculture, transport, banking and trade. The only sector of the economy for which he presented data and figures is a foreign trade. He mentioned that the absorption capacity of a domestic market significantly increased, and that the value of foreign trade increased sevenfold.

However, he failed to draw the conclusion that this was an inevitable sign of economic prosperity. Therefore, it is not surprise that his overall evaluation of the Austro-Hungarian rule in Bosnia and Herzegovina is negative.

2. Foreign historians
   In his monography "The Habsburg Monarchy" Alen J.P. Taylor briefly addressed the Austro-Hungarian governing of Bosnia and Herzegovina. He is highly critical and has an extremely negative assessment of the Monarchy's performance in Bosnia and Herzegovina. Taylor claims that even the most ardent admirers of the Austro-Hungarian Monarchy admit that thirty years of its rule was not to be respected, not for health service, nor railways of normal gauge. There were not state schools nor self-government, even in villages. Some blamed the undefined status of the two provinces. According to Ehrenthal, who was critical of his predecessor Andrassy, things would be different had Bosnia and Herzegovina been annexed, instead of only occupied. If Bosnia and Herzegovina had become part of the Empire it would have got its Diet, schools, trade unions, land reform, roads, and railways. Ehrenthal was an advocate of "the Austrian idea" and had plans to build a railway through the Turkish territory to the Adriatic Sea. Taylor claims that this was an unrealistic and unfeasible project. Its only purpose was to show that Erenthal was a man of progressive ideas.

Bosnia and Herzegovina were not annexed for thirty years and could not be a part of the Monarchy. In a way, the two provinces were a glue of the Monarchy, the only place where "the common Monarchy" was territorially respected. In Taylor's opinion Bosnia and Herzegovina were "the white man's burden" for the Empire. The other European countries sent to their colonies in Africa what Austro-Hungary sent to Bosnia and Herzegovina; a surplus of intellectuals, constructors, developers, archeologists, ethno-graphs, and even rentiers. The two provinces got all the welfare of the emperor's rule: pompous public buildings, immaculate barracks for the occupational army, banks, hotels, coffee shops, and resorts where administrative staff was taking holidays after hard work they did for the Monarchy. But, the real fruits of the Austro-Hungarian governing were absent. In 1918 there were still 88% of illiterate inhabitants in the two provinces. According to Taylor, being fearful of the South Slav nationalism, the Empire clamped down on education and self-management.

Taylor claims that the annexation in 1908 did not help in bringing "The Austrian Idea" to Bosnia and Herzegovina. The annexation did not bring economic improvement, nor new schools, but only more soldiers and bureaucrats. Bosnia and Herzegovina got a Diet, similar to the ones which already existed in the Austrian provinces. There was only a limited voting right for a Diet, which performed only taxing administrative tasks. Taylor points out that in such a system Moslem landowners had two times more
representatives, and that the Habsburg's rule kept a Serbo-Croat majority subdued.
"The Austrian Idea" promised huge improvements, and delivered little. After 1909 Viennese theoreticians gave up on poor and illiterate peasants in Bosnia and Herzegovina.

Taylor did not support his statements with evidence. He neither provided empirical data, which would corroborate his conclusions, nor did he conduct analysis which would come up with advantages and disadvantages of the Austro-Hungarian rule in Bosnia and Herzegovina. Although he is a celebrated and distinguished historian, his one-sided assessment of the Austro-Hungarian period in Bosnia and Herzegovina cannot be taken seriously.

Noel Malcolm points out that dissatisfaction of Christian peasants towards the Austro-Hungarian rule stemmed from the fact that a dual Monarchy applied the policy of continuation and graduality in regards of the question of the land reform. The reform undertaken in 1859 by the Ottoman authorities remained in place and the new authorities were reluctant to make any radical changes. Cosmetic measures were implemented with a view of improvement of the peasant's position. Experts were appointed to estimate the harvest and ten-year average was used as a basis for collecting tenths in order to curb the landowners' abuses of the peasants. Between 1879 and 1913 one third of the peasants managed to buy off the land and liberate themselves from the landlords' bondage. As a result, the Bosnian peasant lived better compared to the Dalmatian or Sicilian peasant, as witnessed by William Miller, the British historian who visited Bosnia and Herzegovina in the 1890s (Malcolm).

According to Malcolm, although Austro-Hungary was reluctant to undertake radical changes, it was eager to apply energetic measures to stimulate economic development. A serious impediment to this effort was the law passed in Vienna in 1880 according to which all expenditures in Bosnia and Herzegovina should be covered by the revenue collected in the country. In other to make more space for dynamic growth and finance building, new infrastructure state loans were approved. In the first two years a railway track 190 kilometers long was built from the Croatian border to Zenica. In the next three years this was extended to link

Zenica with Sarajevo, adding 80 kilometers of new track. A volume of state investment was colossal: until 1907 the government built 111 kilometers of the wide-gauge railway track, 911 kilometers of the narrow-gauge railway track and more than 1,000 KM of main roads, the same number of KM of local roads, and 121 bridge. According to Edith Durham's travelogue in 1906, mountain roads in Bosnia and Herzegovina could match the best one in the most developed European countries (Malcolm).

Malcolm points out that some of these roads and railways were built for military purposes. Nevertheless, they boosted an overall economic development. In addition to infrastructure, Austro-Hungary was very active in exploiting rich natural resources in other to stimulate forestry and mining. He emphasis mining of chromium and copper, and iron ore, resulting in building foundries and steelworks, and several factories of chemical products. In 1912, and 1913 Bosnia and Herzegovina recorded exports of $28 million, and employment of more than 65,000 manufacturing industry workers. Women were also employed in light industry, mainly Christian. In Sarajevo they were employed in a tobacco factory and a carpet factory. The working class expanded, resulting in the establishment of trade unions, which organized a strike in 1906 (Malcolm).

Malcolm claims that the Austro-Hungarian authorities did not neglect agriculture, which was the most important pillar of the Bosnian economy. New experimental agricultural estates vineyards, and ponds were open. Village teachers were taught modern methods, and agricultural school was opened at Ilidza, near Sarajevo. However, the peasants were not familiar with new methods. They were used to old Ottoman roads and loading cattle rather than loading carts. In Herzegovina, the peasants refused to buy iron plugs, which the authorities offered them below cost of production. (Malcolm)

Malcolm praises the Austro-Hungarian education policy. He points out that every religious community had their own schools, financed by the government. He is critical of Yugoslav historians who played down the role of the Austro-Hungarian authorities in promoting education, claiming that only a minority of children attended schools. In order to corroborate his positive assessment of the Austro-Hungarian education policy Malcolm states that one could not say that the authorities did not care about education if they opened 200 primary schools, three secondary schools, a technical school, and a teachers' school, and introduced compulsory primary education in 1909. He quotes the British historian William Miller, who concluded that nobody could have forced parents to send children to school if their parents had wanted to keep them in the darkness of ignorance. (Malcolm)

As a historian Malcolm did not dip into nuances of the Austro-Hungarian economic policy in Bosnia and Herzegovina, or economic theories which backed them. Also, he did not analyze different imbalances in economic development between different regions and different sectors of the economy, which might be the subject of criticism. Nevertheless, he corroborated his statements with data, to arrive at a very positive assessment of the Austro-Hungarian period in Bosnia and Herzegovina. In that respect he approves of the annexation of Bosnia and Herzegovina in 1908, claiming that it brought positive changes. Bosnia and Herzegovina got a constitution and a Parliament, and although voting was limited it enabled the establishment of the real political parties. (Malcolm)

Marko Attila Hoare claims that embryonic industrialization of Bosnia and Herzegovina which started in the last decades of the Ottoman rule could not proceed at a full speed due to a chronic backwardness of the Ottoman state, but had to wait for the Austria-Hungarian government. Austria-Hungary enforced energetically dynamic growth of industry, obviously shaped according to its interests. Two thousand of roads were built only in the first two years of the Austro-Hungarian rule. Bosnian state capital was mobilized by the Bosnian government, with the help of loans floated in Austria-Hungary and on the European capital markets, to build railways and exploit the country's resources in timber and mineral. As a result of this, Bosnian extractive and manufacturing industry gradually developed (Hoare).

The Bosnian government wanted to industrialize the country in order to make it financially self-sufficient and to win the political loyalty of the population. The government encouraged private entrepreneurs to set businesses and then nationalized them in order to establish control of the Bosnian industry. The government, which possessed monopolies in salt and tobacco, established first modern salt-works at Simin Han in 1884, and at Kreka in 1892. It also established tobacco factories in at Sarajevo and Mostar in 1880, at Banjaluka in 1888 and at Travnik in 1893. The state-owned coal mines were opened at Kreka in 1885, at Banjaluka in 1897, at Kakanj in 1900, at Mostar in 1905, and at Breza in 1907. Zenica and Vares became the centers of the country's iron industry after the government opened ironworks in these towns, with the assistance of Austrian capital. The government also opened two chemical factories at Lukavac. The construction of railways accompanied industrial development. It sped the flow of goods across the country by six to eight times. The government granted a concession to the Bavarian industrialist Otto Steinbeis in 1982 to develop a timber factory, which became the largest employer of labor in Bosnia and Herzegovina by the eve of World War I (Hoare).

Hoare's assessment of the Austro-Hungarian rule in Bosnia and Herzegovina is extremely positive. Apart from plentiful data on vigorous industrial development, Hoare particularly emphasized its positive side effect, namely the creation of the labor movement and its internationalist, cosmopolitan character. Croats were disproportionately represented in the labor movement. However, industrial workers belonged to many nationalities and ethnicities; apart from the three major ethnic groups, there were Czechs, Poles, Germans, Hungarians, Slovenes and Jews. Drvar, predominantly Serb town in northwestern part of Bosnia, became the country's center of a timber industry. It attracted many skilled workers from almost all parts of the Austro-Hungarian empire. This was the basis of establishment of multiethnic and multinational trade unions, which became a bulwark against the sectarian trends among workers, which were encouraged by some nationalistic political leaders. (Hoare)

Sarajevo, as the country's capital, became industrial center of the country with highest concentration of the labor movement organizations. The population of the city increased by 143% in a period 1879-1910 to reach 52,000, compared to Banjaluka, whose population grew by 55% in the same period to reach 15,000, and Tuzla, whose population grew by 121%, to reach slightly more than 11,000 inhabitants. Forty-five% of

Sarajevo's civilian population were immigrants, three quarters of them not native speakers of the Serbo-Croat language. This made Sarajevo almost as cosmopolitan and multinational as Vienna, and most cosmopolitan and most multinational in all the Yugoslav lands.

Sarajevo's domination of the labor movement surpassed its proportion in the industry of Bosnia and Herzegovina. On the eve of WWI, the city gave two thirds of trade union members and members of the Social Democratic Party of Bosnia and Herzegovina (Hoare).

Hoare positively assesses the annexation of Bosnia and Herzegovina in 1908. It enabled further unification of the labor movement in the Western South Slav lands. As a result of removal of legal obstacles, which existed before the annexation, the Social Democratic parties of Slovenia, Croatia, and Bosnia and Herzegovina convened at a joint conference in Ljubljana in November 1909. The conference resolved in a favor of a single "Yugoslav nation", and the unification of all South Slav lands as a single state-unity within the Habsburgs Monarchy. The Social Democratic Party of Bosnia and Herzegovina, therefore, declared itself for the national unity of the Yugoslavs, and consequently of all Serbs, Croats and Muslims. It opposed the curial voting system, which divided electorate in Bosnia and Herzegovina along religious lines, and which kept the Social Democratic Party out of the Bosnian Sabor in the Austro-Hungarian period (Hoare).

Robin Okey states that in a memorandum to the European great powers of 21st April 1878 the Austro-Hungarian foreign minister Gyula Andrassy made a case for the Habsburg occupation of Bosnia and Herzegovina. He pointed out that Bosnia and Herzegovina was not equipped for autonomous development. A great power was therefore needed to bring prosperity, the rule of law, and above everything to carry out a cultural mission in the country which was as backward as some of European external colonies after more than four centuries of the Ottoman rule. Behind these altruistic outpours a high policy is easily revealed. By occupying Bosnia and Herzegovina and in the view of the Russian victory over the Ottoman Empire in 1877, Austro-Hungary wanted to curb Slav nationalism and prevent the formation of a large South Slav state.

The best person to carry out the Empire's mission was Benjamin von Kallay. A descendant of Hungarian nobility, brought up by a Hungarianized Serb mother, Kallay was an expert in Serb affairs. He was the Empire's Consul General in Belgrade from 1868 to 1874. During this period Kallay tried to forge the alliance between Serbs and Hungarians, revolved around the plan of the establishment of 'The Danubian Confederation'. He also wrote a book 'The *History of Serbs in Bosnia and Herzegovina*', which he later renounced.

Kallay's administration of Bosnia and Herzegovina marks the longest period of the Austro-Hungarian occupation of Bosnia and Herzegovina from its beginning in 1878 to his death in 1903. The main characteristic of his strategy was the promotion of the Bosnian nationhood. By doing this Kallay wanted to cushion Serb and Croat nationalism and facilitate a smooth integration of the province in the Empire. History textbooks paid a special attention to history of the medieval Bosnian kingdom with the view of raising the Bosnian national conscience. Kallay treated the Slav population of Bosnia and Herzegovina as Bosnians of three faiths. Religious and cultural autonomy was promoted to emphasize religious, rather than national sentiments among Serbs and Croats. Kallay regarded Bosnian beys as the pillar of such a strategy considering them the descendants of medieval Bosnian Bogumil aristocracy. However, he did not abandon hopes that Muslims, detached from an Islamic superpower, will eventually return to Christianity.

Kallay was replaced by Istvan Burian, who governed Bosnia and Herzegovina from 1903 to 1912. During this period cultural institutions among all the three communities mushroomed. Burian was also seeking rapprochement to Serbs. This was not the result of his Serbo-philia, but a pragmatic approach aimed at diverting Bosnian and Herzegovinian Serbs from Serbia. At the same time Burian intensified government control of cultural and educational institutions, which made him unpopular, especially among Serbs.

Burian was replaced by Oskar von Potiorek in 1912. In his policy he combined a long-term strategic goal of crushing Serbia with an attempt to attract as many Serbs as possible in political life, especially in the Diet.

In a general assessment of the Austro-Hungarian policy in Bosnia and Herzegovina Professor Okey recognized that the Empire had faced an awesome task in its mission. He stated that its policy of economic and industrial development was relatively successful, although the unresolved agrarian question (it was also unresolved in many other parts of the Empire, e.g, Hungary) left a vast majority of the peasants in abject poverty with their standard of living almost stagnant.

Professor Okey gives more credit to the Empire's educational policy. State-backed common schools for all the three communities established a long lasting basis for the integration of the Bosnian communities. The biggest success derived from such an educational policy was the emergence of a small educated Muslim elite imbibing the Western system of values to its community. In historical perspective this laid grounds to the evolution of the modern Bosniac nation.

Professor Okey's assessment of the Austro-Hungarian national policy is less favorable. He states that Kallay overestimated his skills and that promotion of a Bosnian nation and denial of Serbdom and Croatdom in Bosnia was like a red rag to a bull.

In his overall assessment of the Austro-Hungarian record in Bosnia and Herzegovina Professor Okey makes comparison with the period of a communist rule. Similar in duration the both periods witnessed relative economic prosperity and progress in education. However, the both system of governing failed to solve the national question.

Austro-Hungarian administration in Bosnia and Herzegovina faced two irresoluble problems. Its civilizing mission ran out of steam when Serb and Croat nationalists embraced the European system of values. They claimed that their quest for modernity and prosperity was more valid since it excluded an alien rule. Second, promotion of civic versus ethnic nationalism was contested by Serb and Croat nationalist. Serb and Croat intellectuals and burgeoning bourgeois class, as bearers of national conscience, claimed that their nationalism was civic and not ethnic, by treating all the three communities as Serbs and Croats of three faiths respectively. The Empires administrators realized that they were not dealing with backward Orientals of three faiths but with a modern nationalism of the Central European type. Eventually, the Austro-Hungarian Empire as a supra-national entity lost its appeal and was replaced after the World War I by nation states which could cater better for collective identities of their constituent peoples.

In his evaluation of the Austro-Hungarian rule in Bosnia and Herzegovina Okey covered almost all the relevant economic, social, national and educational aspects. His approach is unbiased, unemotional and scientific. He emphasized successes and failures of the Austro-Hungarian administration in an objective manner of an outstanding scholar.

3. Domestic economists

Kemal Hrelja starts his analysis of industrialization of Bosnia and Herzegovina during the Austro-Hungarian period with paraphrasing Lenin: "*The famous Lenin's statement that imperialist powers first build railways and then via them send generals, missionaries, and capital, was completely confirmed in the case of Bosnia and Herzegovina. Immediately after the occupation building of railways commenced. They were used to import a ready-made manufacturing industry from the Austro-Hungary."* (Hrelja)

> Hrelja states that the state and foreign private capital had received economic and legal privileges in establishing manufacturing industries which would produce raw materials for the manufacturing industry in the core country, namely forest industry, mining, and chemical industry. Bosnia and Herzegovina served as an outlet for unemployed capital and the market for the final products made in the center of the Monarchy. In addition, tobacco, graphic, and small carpet and embroidery work shops were opened with a view of employing poor city dwellers and make the new regime popular among native population. (Hrelja)

> Industries built in the last two decades of the nineteenth century were of a low technological level. In-spite of this they were profitable due to a mixture of favorable factors such as almost free raw materials, lower transport tariffs, tax relief, cheap workforce, and the membership in monopolistic cartels. The technological level of some of these industries such as forest industry, mining, ironworks, steelworks, tobacco and chemical industry was significantly increased at the beginning of the twentieth century due to increased competition in domestic and world market. As a result, productivity increased significantly, despite the fact that the number of workers decreased and the working day was reduced from 13 to 9.5 hours. Hrelja noticed that industries which were not export-oriented such as construction, textile and food industry had not experienced technological improvement, which is

according to him the best proof of the colonial status of the domestic manufacturing industry. (Hrelja)

Hrelja provided a detailed analysis of micro and macro location of the Bosnian industry. He noticed that very often the main factor in determination of industry location was a closeness to sources of raw materials, while other factors such as closeness to the market or availability of workforce were ignored. Also, political considerations very often had taken a precedence over economic rationale. As a result, technological progress was impeded by the lack of space of industry expansion. Macro factors of location were determined by short-term profit motives, and not by a coherent long-term strategy. This led to industry concentration in big towns which were connected by railways. As a result, large swathes of land were left without transportation infrastructure and manufacturing industry. (Hrelja)

Hrelja emphasizes the great economic and social dynamics expressed in the transformation of the economy from a subsistence into a monetary one, building industrial enterprises, and creation of the working class, whose number amounted to 100,000 or 6% of the total number of inhabitants. However, all activities had to fit into the interests of the Austrians and Hungarians. So long as these interests coincided with the interests of the native population progress was unquestionable; roads, narrow-gauge, but still efficient railway-net, manufacturing industry, and well-ordered administration. (Hrelja)

However, the peasants saw little improvement. Feudal relationships still persisted, and voluntary buy-out of land went slowly and ended up in serfs being transformed into free peasants with little land in their ownership. Technical improvements did not raise productivity by much due to small plots and a sharp rise of population.

The internal market of Bosnia and Herzegovina was flooded with cheap industrial goods from more developed parts of the Monarchy. This obliterated most of domestic craft industry, although it led to the appearance of new crafts.

Hrelja points out that transformation of society brought by the occupation created a new social dynamics-class grouping and organized political life. Modern bourgeois society was built together with the working class and all the respective political and social consequences. (Hrelja)

Although Hrelja's study is mainly devoted to the industrial development in Bosnia and Herzegovina during the Austro-Hungarian period he briefly analyzed all the aspects of economic life. He skillfully weighs pros and cons of the Austro-Hungarian economic achievements. He is sharp in revealing motives behind actions of the occupation authorities. Although critical to almost every aspect of the Austro-Hungarian management of Bosnia and Herzegovina he does no fall into *a fallacy of composition* trap. His overall assessment is positive, particularly compared to the period which followed the break-up of the Austro-Hungarian Monarchy. During the Austro-Hungarian period, four times more industrial enterprises and four times more kilometers of railway lines were built per year, compared to the period of the Kingdom of Yugoslavia.

Vjekoslav Domljan points out that Austro-Hungary inherited a pastoral economy in Bosnia and Herzegovina, in which 95% of the population lived in villages and drew their income from agriculture. A vigorous industrialization of the country started when Benjamin von Kallay was appointed a common minister of finance. His vision was to increase the standard of living, improve education, introduce political self-government, and make Bosnia and Herzegovina a model Balkan country.

Unprecedented economic growth, unmatched in the history of Bosnia and Herzegovina, started in 1882 when the count Kallay, the greatest reformer in the country's history, introduced industrial and financial institution. (Domljan)

Since Kallay's hands were tied with regards to financing investment by the promise given to the Sultan Abdul Hamid that expenditures had to be financed only by revenue collected in Bosnia and Herzegovina, he decided to embark on the "Keynesian policy"of budget financing. However, this policy was short-lived, and was replaced by the policy of state loans, which were used to finance big infrastructure projects. Relying on the support of the military he modernized roads, introduced the telephone, and build railways. As a result, public debt soared. (Domljan)

Austro-Hungary built 1,684 KM of railway track in Bosnia and Herzegovina. Some of them were of such a quality that they would be admired even in Western Europe.

Developing mining and forestry, without which it was not possible to raise the standard of living, required other sources of finance. In other to attract private capital, which initially did not have interest to invest, Kallay offered private capital grants and privileges. Some decisions were weird, such as a refusal to give the permission to a Czech textile factory to open wool spinning workshop, and the permission for opening paper factory, which in-spite of huge subsidies went bankrupt. Some foreign diplomats accused Kallay for corruption, claiming that he was a partner in all factories. (Domljan)

In the period 1881-1913, the manufacturing industry in Bosnia and Herzegovina rose at an average annual rate of 12.4%, and in 1890s at an average annual rate of 15%. Domljan names this staggering growth an economic miracle. (Domljan)

In 1907 Bosnia and Herzegovina was three times more industrialized than Serbia, and five times more industrialized than Bulgaria.

Manufacturing industry was predominantly state-owned. Sugar factories, breweries, and distilleries were owned by private foreign investors. Small-scale industry prevailed in production of food and clothes. The main characteristic of industrialization of Bosnia and Herzegovina was establishment of private firms and nationalizing them, and developing state capitalism. (Domljan)

The manufacturing industry in Bosnia and Herzegovina was export-oriented, with the predominance of intermediate goods. The main exporting staples were coal, minerals, and raw and semi-processed wood. The Bosnian economy benefitted from the fact that it was a member of the customs union of 53 million people and that its currency was stable. (Domljan)

Domljan undertook an aggregate analysis without delving into structural imbalances which inevitably accompany such a vigorous growth. His assessment of the Austro-Hungarian rule in Bosnia and Herzegovina is extremely positive. In order to corroborate his assessment, he compared 20 years of economic development in the Austro-Hungarian period, independent Bosnia and Herzegovina, and the first and the second Yugoslavia. His conclusion is that the Austro-Hungarian period was the most successful, followed by the current period of independent Bosnia and Herzegovina, the Second Yugoslavia and the First Yugoslavia. (Domljan)

4. Foreign economists

Michael Palairet assesses agriculture performance as poor. Unresolved agricultural questions, inherited from the Ottoman period, demotivated both the landowners and the peasants to invest and increase efficiency. Bosnian agricultural production per capita was much lower than in Bulgaria and Serbia. The standard of living in some rural areas of Bosnia and Herzegovina was higher in the Ottoman period. (Palairet)

Relative neglect of agriculture and focus on building infrastructure and heavy industry Palairet compares with Geschrenkron's explanation of Russia before the World War I. The main characteristic of "top-down" industrialization of Bosnia and Herzegovina was import substitution, accompanied by membership in the Austro-Hungarian customs union, and reliance on government subsidies and foreign capital. This model of industrial development produced a vigorous growth of manufacturing industry. Growth was particularly strong during the Kallay's period (1882-2003), when the growth of the manufacturing industry averaged 15%. Kallay's successor Istvan Byrian significantly reduced subsidies in order to improve public finance. As a result, industrial growth slowed down. Inspite of this manufacturing industry grew at a staggering annual rate of 12.4% in a period 1880-1913. Vigorous industrial growth lifted up the other sectors of the Bosnian economy. Before the WWI Bosnia and Herzegovina was more developed than Russia, Bulgaria and Serbia, and as developed as Italy. (Palairet)

Whilst successful in industrial policy, Austro-Hungary failed in education and health policy. Before World War I, the literacy rate in Bosnia and Herzegovina was only 12.2%, compared to 20.3% in Serbia and 42% in Bulgaria. The number of children attending schools fell by 22% compared to the Ottoman period. Public health was another weak spot as elsewhere in the Monarchy. The child mortality rate was 162/1,000, compared to 140 for Serbia and 159 for Bulgaria.

In conclusion, Palairet places Austro-Hungarian policies in the following order from the bottom to the top; the health policy, the education policy, the agricultural policy, and the industrial policy. Although agriculture was neglected it was more market-oriented compared to Serbia and Bulgaria, and the position of the peasant was less dramatic than in Dalmatia and Sicily. There were not enough banks, but transport and communications were relatively well developed. Wages were higher than in the other Balkan countries, and income per head was lifted up from typically Balkan levels to those in the Central Europe. (Palairet)

Palairet's analysis is thorough, multifaceted, and objective. He used sources in which the authors applied various statistical methods to calculate major macroeconomic indicators, and to enable the comparison between a chosen group of countries. He carefully treaded in emphasizing advantages and disadvantages of the Austro-Hungarian rule in Bosnia and Herzegovina to arrive to an overall positive assessment.

Peter Sugar points out that Austria-Hungary had an overall plan for Bosnia and Herzegovina. Kallay strove to increase in the Bosnians the feeling that they belonged to a great and powerful nation. Austria-Hungary was aware that there was a friction between its interests and political sympathies of the population. In order to switch the populations loyalty from the neighboring states to the Empire political propaganda was not sufficient. A vigorous economic development accompanied by a significant increase in the standard of living was necessary to make their rule attractive to the native population. This was in agreement with what the administration of the province, or at least Kallay, believed to be the mandate which Austria-Hungary got from Europe at the Congress of Berlin. The men who were given the task of taking charge of administration of the province felt that economic progress designed to raise the living standard in Bosnia and Herzegovina best served both the honor of the state and its basic interests. (Sugar)

In their aims to improve the economy of Bosnia and Herzegovina, the planners in Vienna had to resolve two problems; limitation contained in the law of 22 February 1880, which stipulated that the provincial administration had to rely in its affairs only on domestic sources of finance, and the implementation of the comprehensive plan of economic development. To achieve both goals, the administration envisaged a program in three phases; Firstly, they intended to build up the province's economy to the level which would generate additional revenues for the provincial government and more goods and services for the population. Secondly, they had to map out carefully program of mass education, and thirdly to gradually extend political rights of the Monarchy's citizens to the inhabitants of Bosnia and Herzegovina. (Sugar)

Sugar claims that while the double aims of a high living standard and fiscal independence can hardly be criticized its sequence of economic growth, education, and political rights was a reminiscent of the long-range programs of colonial powers and therefore was a mistake. It produced a very strict administrative system which increased the opposition of the politically enlightened element of Bosnia and Herzegovina against Austria-Hungary, in-spite of economic progress and political concessions introduced in 1908. In addition, the second and the third steps were taken very slowly. For example, in 1908 only 15% of the children of school age attended high schools, whose number of 12 was miserably low. Bosnia and Herzegovina had no university, and for political reasons the graduates of her high schools were not permitted to attend universities in Austria-Hungary where instruction was given in a Slav language. This limited the number of university students from the province to those few with an advance knowledge of German or Hungarian. (Sugar)

Sugar points out that the economic development programs cannot be carried out unless the traditional and cultural factors are taken into consideration also. All these factors, including the economic, must be brought into harmony with each other. This is something Austria-Hungary failed to realize. The best proof for this is not only related to the three aforementioned elements of the program but also to the authorities' treatment of the religious institutions, by their attempt to create the Bosnian nationality, and by the exclusion of the local population from not only administrative posts, but also from participation in economic enterprise. By concentrating for the first thirty years of the occupation almost exclusively on the economic facets of development, the Austro-Hungarian government neglected other complex aspects of life which proved to be no less important than economic prosperity. (Sugar)

Sugar draws parallels between industrialization of Bosnia and Herzegovina in the Austro-Hungarian period and industrialization of the Soviet Union in the 1920s and 1930s. The striking similarity between the two industrialization programs stems from their two main characteristics; neglect of agriculture, and focus on heavy industry. In the absence of a strong and expanding domestic market which would support a growth of manufacturing industry a development of heavy industry relies on subsidies, grants and tariff protection, all of this a heavy burden on public finance.

Sugar stresses that the failure of agrarian reforms stems from the fact that their aim is redistribution of wealth rather than its creation. Looking at Bosnia and Herzegovina one could spot two mistakes in agrarian reforms; firstly, they were delayed for political reason, secondly, when they were introduced they were motivated by political and not economic reasons. As a consequence, the expected results were not achieved. (Sugar)

Quoting Arthur Lewis, the Nobel prize winner in Economics, Sugar states that the main weakness in agrarian moves in Bosnia and Herzegovina was that they clashed with the peasants' tradition and culture. Extensive use of large-scale projects only antagonized the usually conservative peasantry. To corroborate this statement Sugar mentions the failure of the four agricultural stations which were established in Bosnia and Herzegovina between 1886 and 1893 to teach the peasantry improved methods. Peasants should have been trained new methods on their farms, and if they had succeeded it was likely that their neighbors would have followed their example. Unfortunately, the Austro-Hungarians never thought of using peasants directly in their efforts aimed at the introduction of new methods and crops into their province. In a nutshell, the Austro-Hungarians made a mistake in thinking that they could transplant the established value system which prevailed in the Dual Monarchy, overlooking that the relationships between the various segments of the population was hostile, social mobility was almost nonexistent, and rural underemployment was a great problem. (Sugar)

Sugar claims that he is not acquainted with theories of economic development, although his analysis proves otherwise. He admits that "induced growth" is necessary in underdeveloped economy for a period of a couple of decades. However, this stage needs to lay grounds for a sustained growth. This had never happened in Bosnia and Herzegovina which failed to enter the Rostow's stage of "take-off".

Sugar quotes the famous German economist Walter Hoffman, whose research had shown that in an early stage of industrialization consumer industry prevails, while in the mature stage of industrialization capital goods industry takes over. Sugar admits that implementation of the inverse Hoffman model was justified in Bosnia and Herzegovina considering its rich natural resources in minerals, ores and forests, He also accepts the need to put heavy industry under state ownership. However, Sugar is very critical of the same trend in light industry. The state involvement and exclusion of local and foreign entrepreneurs from designing light industrial policy produced poor results in food and beverages, textile, and leather industry. Government mismanagement caused a bankruptcy of several companies in these industries. (Sugar)

Sugar is highly critical of the Austro-Hungarian transportation policy. The transportation system did not develop in a manner which could have helped the development of its economy. The country was not connected with a good seaport, with the rest of the Balkans, nor with Austria. Hungary had the upper hand in designing the Bosnia and Herzegovina transportation network.

In designing the transportation system political considerations had a primacy in comparison with economic rationale. Railways network was built in a haphazard manner in the early 1880s, although most of the future mining and industrial sites were already known. Sugar thinks that Austria-Hungary cannot be blamed for keeping the railways under the management of the authorities, but must be criticized for not having run the railways in the interest of over-all development. Aiming to earn profits from the railways, the provincial government's tariff policy contributed to pricing out the provinces ores out of the world market. At the same time it limited rail shipments to the extent that it had difficulties to break even. If the aim of the railways system was to make profit, then it should have been given to private companies, if they were owned by the state they should have been treated as public utilities. (Sugar)

After criticizing almost all aspects of the authorities' economic policy one would expect a slating overall evaluation of the Austro-Hungarian rule in Bosnia and Herzegovina. Nothing of the sort. After conducting such a thorough and deep analysis Sugar could not have been one-sided and fall in *pars pro toto*/the fallacy of the composition trap. In a sudden twist, resembling suspense thrillers, Sugar wraps up his analysis with a favorable overall evaluation of the Monarchy's role in Bosnia and Herzegovina:

"It is very unlikely that the men in Vienna and Sarajevo who directed the affairs of Bosnia and Herzegovina used the criteria employed so far in this chapter when they attempted to evaluate the results of their efforts. It is even less likely that their analyses would have produced the more or less unfavorable balance sheet presented by this chapter. It is much more likely that they would have pointed with pride to theirs far from negligible achievements. Bosnia and Herzegovina were, certainly, more advanced in 1918 than she had been before the troops of the Habsburgs occupied the territory. The province enjoyed thirty-six years of peace interrupted only by the insurrection of 1882, while the other Balkan people fought several wars during the same period. Law and order were maintained during these years by the authorities, and under these favorable circumstances the province was able to develop. The Austro-Hungarians left behind them a good network of roads, a few railroads, and some factories when they withdrew. These, together with the numerous public buildings and the introduction of utilities such as water works, and street lights which were built in most towns, represented real and permanent gains for Bosnia and Herzegovina. Most of these buildings, power plants, water works, and similar structures are still in use or are still operating today serving the present-day inhabitants of the old province of the Dual Monarchy."............"The authorities undoubtedly succeeded in improving the living conditions in Bosnia and Herzegovina by improving transportation, by raising the revenue of the plum growers of the Posavina, by making coal available to an ever-increasing number of people, by the new job opportunities which the various industries created, and by the slow but increasing transformation of the serfs into free peasants." (Sugar)

To conclude, this literature review leads to three conclusions:

1. Evaluation of the Austro-Hungarian period in Bosnia and Herzegovina ranges from extremely negative (Taylor) to extremely positive (Domljan)

2. With this exception, the evaluation of the foreign authors is more favorable compared to the assessment of the domestic authors

3. More exact analysis, corroborated with facts and figures, results in more favorable evaluation of the Austro-Hungarian rule in Bosnia and Herzegovina.

CHAPTER FOUR

METHODOLOGY

The authors, when discussing economic matters, use figures and numbers to corroborate their statements. These numbers are of two types;

1. Physical, such as the length of railway network, the number of KM of roads, production of agricultural and industrial goods, or the number of workers employed, and;

2. Monetary such as the value of production, the level of foreign trade, the amount of banking capital or the level of workers' wages.

However, apart from Palairet and Domljan, the authors do not use macroeconomic indicators such as GDP, GDP per capita, or rate of growth of GDP. These three indicators are vital in macroeconomic analysis. For with all its drawbacks, GDP shows the size of an economy, GDP per capita the standard of living, while the rate of growth of GDP shows a dynamism of an economy and a success of economic policy measures. This is why in sectoral analysis of the Bosnian economy these indicators will be used and, if not given, calculated, provided that available data allow it.

Economic variables such as GDP, population, inflation, and interest rate grow at a geometric progression. In other words, they have exponential growth, since they rise at a compound rate. [3] There are several formulae related to a compound rate:

---

[3] The power of exponential growth is best illustrated by the legend related to the origin of the game of chess. The legend goes that an Indian called Sisa Ben Dahir invented chataranga, the chess game whose rules were slightly different from the rules of the

1. Factor 72. It is used to calculate the number of years in which one variable will approximately double when it grows at a compound rate.

   $n_2 = 72/g$,

   where n_2 is the number of years in which a variable will double and g is a growth rate

   The formula can be obtained in the following way:

   The double time of a variable which grows with the g% annual rate can be calculated with a formula $(1 + g/100) = 2$. Taking natural logarithm on both sides of the equation we arrive at n x ln $(1 + g/100)$ 0 ln 2. Natural logarithm of $(1 + g/100) = g/100$, while natural logarithm of 2 is approximately 0.72. Multiplying both sides with 100 we arrive at our formula. (Mahmutefendic) (1)

2. Factor 109 It is used to calculate the number of years in which one variable will approximately triple when it grows at a compound rate.

   $n_3 = 108/g$,

   where n_3 is the number of years in which a variable will triple and g is a growth rate

---

modern chess. He went to a raja's court and showed him the game. The raja was delighted with the invention and wanted to reward Sisa Ben Dahir. Sisa Ben Dahir asked him to give him one grain of wheat on the first square of the chess board, two grains on the second square, four on the third one and so one. "Such a modest reward for such a beautiful game", the raja said. Sisa Ben Dahir insisted in his "modest wish". The raja sent his emissaries around the country. They returned in shock. There was not enough wheat to satisfy "the modest wish" in an entire kingdom. Later it was found out that the amount Sisa Ben Dahir required had been equal to a ten-year world wheat output in 1964. The number of grains which would cover the whole chess board at the geometric progression is equal to $2^{64}-1$. (Bjelica)

The formula can be obtained in the following way:

The triple time of a variable which grows with the g% annual rate can be calculated with a formula $(1 + g/100) = 3$. Taking natural logarithm on both sides of the equation we arrive at $n \times \ln(1 + g/100) = \ln 3$. Natural logarithm of $(1 + g/100) = g/100$, while natural logarithm of 3 is approximately 108. Multiplying both sides with 100 we arrive at our formula (Owen J, Haese R, Haese S, Bruce M) (2)

3. Factor 144 It is used to calculate the number of years in which one variable will approximately quadruple when it grows at a compound rate.

$n_4 = 144/g$,

where n_3 is the number of years in which a variable will triple and g is a growth rate

The formula can be obtained in the following way:

The quadruple time of a variable which grows with the g% annual rate can be calculated with a formula $(1 + g/100) = 4$. Taking natural logarithm on both sides of the equation we arrive at $n \times \ln(1 + g/100) = \ln 4$. Natural logarithm of $(1 + g/100) = g/100$, while natural logarithm of 43 is approximately 144. Multiplying both sides with 100 we arrive at our formula (3)

4. In the same way we can derive the formulae for five-fold, six-fold, seven-fold, eight-fold, nine-fold, ten-fold, eleven-fold, twelve-fold, thirteen-fold, fourteen-fold, fifteen-fold, and sixteen-fold increase in GDP or any other variable: five-fold factor is 162, six-fold factor is 180, seven-fold factor is 198, eight-fold factor is 216,

nine-fold factor is 225, ten-fold factor is 234, eleven-fold factor is 243, twelve-fold factor is 252, thirteen-fold factor is 261, fourteen-fold factor is 270, fifteen-fold factor is 279, and sixteen-fold factor is 288.

5. It is possible to derive the formula for calculating how many times a variable increased over actual a period of time:

    $N = 2^{na/n}$,

    Where N stands for the number of times a variable increased over an actual period of time,

    na for an actual number of years,

    and n for the number of years in which the variable doubles

6. Δ GDP – the percentage change in GDP. From the formula (1) we can derive the following formula for calculating the change in GDP:

    Δ GDP = n x g x 100/72

    Where Δ GDP stands for the change in GDP

    n for the number of years observed

    g for the growth rate, and

    100/72 for the compounding fact (4)

7. Δ GDP – the percentage change in GDP. If the number of years in which we calculate increase in GDP

exceeds the number of years in which this increase doubles then we can use the following formula:

$$\Delta \text{GDP} = n_2 \times g \times 100/72 \times (1 + g)^{n - n_2},$$

Where n stands for the number of years for which a change in GDP needs to be calculated, and

n_2 stands for the number of years in which GDP doubles.[4]

8. g – the growth rate. From the formula (4) we can derive the formula for calculating the growth rate:

$$g \times 100/72 = \Delta \text{GDP}/n$$

$$g = \Delta \text{GDP}/n \times 72/100 \quad (5)$$

9. $\Delta \text{GDP}/Y$ – the percentage change in GDP. There is an alternative, more complicated way to calculate the percentage change in GDP, which is supposed to give the same result:

$$\Delta Y = Y (1 + g)^n - Y$$

$$\Delta Y = Y ((1 + g)^n - 1) \quad (6)$$

10. g – the growth rate. From the formula (6) we can derive the formula for calculating the growth rate:
$$\Delta Y = Y ((1 + g)^n - 1)$$

---

[4] For example, if we want to calculate the percentage increase in GDP in 12 years when an average annual growth rate of GDP is 7.2%, we will get $n_2 = 72/g = 72/7.2 = 10$; Δ GDP = $10 \times 7.2 \times 100/72 \times (1 + 0.072)^{12-10} = 100 \times (1 + 1.072)^2 = 100 \times 1.15 = 115\%$ increase in GDP.

$$\Delta Y/Y = (1 + g)^n - 1$$

$$\Delta Y/Y + 1 = (1 + g)^n$$

$$(\Delta Y + Y)/Y = (1 + g)^n$$

$$((\Delta Y + Y)/Y)^{1/n} = 1 + g$$

$$g = ((\Delta Y + Y)/Y)^{1/n} - 1 \quad (7)$$

11. g – the growth rate. We can also calculate the growth rate in the following way:

    $\Delta Y = Y((1+g)^n - 1)/Y;\ \Delta Y/Y = ((1+g)^n - 1);\ \Delta Y/Y + 1 = (1+g)^n;\ \Delta Y + Y/Y = (1+g)^n.$

    We can logarithm both sides of the equation and arrive at: $\log(\Delta Y + Y) - \log Y = n \log(1+g)/n;\ (\log(\Delta Y + Y) - \log Y)/n = \log(1+g);\ 1 + g = 10^{((\log \Delta Y + Y) - \log Y)/n};\ g = 10^{((\log \Delta Y + Y) - \log Y)/n} - 1$

12. – Inflation. In a similar way inflation can be calculated:

    $= n \times p \times 100/72 \quad (8)$

    Where stands for inflation over a period of n years, n for the number of years, p for the annual rate of inflation, and 100/72 for compounding factor

13. p – annual rate of inflation. From the formula (8) we can derive the formula for calculating the annual rate of inflation:

    $p = /n \times 72/100 \quad (9)$

CHAPTER FIVE

SECTORAL ANALYSIS OF THE ECONOMY OF BOSNIA AND HERZEGOVINA

AGRICULTURE

a) Farming

Austro-Hungary inherited feudal agricultural relations from the Ottoman Empire. Land reform and land tenure remained a cancer in a tissue of the Bosnian economy and society and the biggest problem for the local population and the new authorities. This issue was never resolved, and although it was considered for the entire period of the Austro-Hungarian administration only once was a change introduced. This was the tax reform of 1905 which was not received favorably and was not accepted as a solution by the population.

The Christian serfs working for Muslim landlords expected radical changes from the new Christian ruling power when Austria-Hungary took over the country. They expected sweeping expropriation of the beys and agas. Waiting for this to happen they refused to work. In the response the government had to issue a warning that it was going to collect all taxes irrespective of the peasantry's income to force them to return to work. (Sugar)

The government offered several explanations as an excuse for the postponement of the solution of the agrarian question. Firstly, the authorities argued that without a cadaster a change in landholding was not possible, and that without this record it was also impossible to convert the tithe into a land tax. But more essential reasons lay in the fact that the authorities invoked the principle of respect for private property, whose violation would lead to an unequal treatment of religions by expropriation of Muslim landlords in favor of the Christian peasantry. In addition, the landlords not knowing how to handle money would soon be penniless if the government paid them for the land handed over to the serfs and therefore the government would be burdened with a paramount problem of providing for thousands of destitute families. (Sugar)

Although this argument looks plausible, behind it loomed another problem. According to the law of 22 February 1880, Bosnia and Herzegovina had to be financially self-supporting. The expenses of administration were ever rising and about one-third of the fiscal income came from the tithe.

The political considerations were also taken into account by the authorities. The Common Minister of Finance had to act in agreement with the two governments of Austria and Hungary. Powerful Hungarian landowners, who dominated the Hungarian Parliament, would certainly not approved of a dangerous precedence which could have triggered the rebellion of the Hungarian peasants and their eventual expropriation. Furthermore, the authorities new that they had the support of Catholic Croats, but not Christian Orthodox Serbs. Therefore, they needed the support of the Muslim community, whose pillar were the landowners, in other to secure a pro-Austro-Hungarian majority in Bosnia and Herzegovina. It was obvious that radical land reform would make them the enemies of the monarchy. (Sugar)

Apart from the principles and economic and political considerations, the problem lied, as the French consul S. Auzepy noticed in 1892, in the fact that the agrarian problem was misunderstood in Vienna. The impression was that the landowners were unwilling to sell their land, which was not true. They would have been happy to sell it if they could have found the buyers. Also, the government was wrong in its claim that the peasants did not know how to run their farms once they bought them, and went bankrupt within a short time. The problem was that the serfs did not have the money to buy land, and when they got it they were short of working capital. The cause of all evil was still the tithe. The government officials were greedy and corrupt. Their assessment of the harvest was so high that the tithe normally amounted to 20% instead of legally 10%. The serf then had to pay the assessed tax in cash in the early autumn before he could sell his harvest profitably. In terms of modern economic theory one could say that Adam Smith's principles of taxation were grossly violated. The serf could not complain and had to borrow the money either from the landowner or from the loan sharks. Understandably, the loans were short-term and interest rates were astronomic. The serf had to sell his harvest fast, at any price, in order to repay his loan with interest in time. The government could address this problem by checking on tax collectors, loan sharks and dates on which taxes were collected. (Sugar)

Theoretically, Kallay had these measures at his disposal. Firstly, he could have clamped down on corruption, which he did to a certain extent (Kapidzic). The second measure was unknown at the time since it came into existence with the Keynesian revolution, namely automatic stabilizers and fine tuning. For example, during bad harvests the tithe could have been reduced to 5%, and one third paid to the landowner to one fifth, while during good harvests the tithe could have been increased to let's say 12-15%, and one third to the landowner to let's say two fifths. This would overall increased the tax revenue and at the same time brought a relief to the peasants.

However, Kallay was proud of his achievement in improving agriculture. He used statistics to show that the stories about the misery of the serf are not true, and that they lived better than ever before. He pointed out that between 1879 and 1895 the agricultural population rose by 37% and the number of houses in rural districts rose by 39%. He added that the number of animals increased 158% and that agricultural production in

1895 was 156% of that in 1879. Although these figures look impressive they conceal some other factors which make the picture he painted much less rosy. He did not mention that this impressive growth in agricultural production was the result of a low base in 1879, much lower than in 1874 because of the peasants' uprising which destroyed many houses, many animals, and had damaged many fields. Kallay also failed to mention that while the agricultural population increased by 37%, the tithe increased by 101% from 2,089,844 florins in 1880 to 4,202,000 florins in 1895 and that beside the tithe the peasants also paid new taxes which did not exist in 1879. However, the budget of 1895 called for only 3,858,000 florins in tithe payments compared to 3,524,212 in 1875. (Sugar)

A bit of algebra might help to clarify things. When many countries adopted the gold standard in 1870, the inflation rate unified across the countries. World experienced deflation in the period 1870-1896. According to some research an average annual inflation rate in this period was -0.86% (Gerlach & Stuart). Using our formula (8) we can calculate cumulative inflation in this period:

$$= n \times p \times 100/72$$

$$= 20 \times (-0.86) \times 100/72 = -17.20 \times 100/72 = 24$$

This means that prices were 24% lower in 1895 compared to 1875. In order to calculate the purchasing power of the tithe in 1895 expressed in 1875 prices we can set the following proportion:

3, 858,000: (100-24) = X:100

Solving this proportion and rounding figures off we arrive at the figure of 5,1 million florins of tithes in 1895 in real terms.

Now, we can calculate the GDP growth in farming in the period 1875-1895:

(5,100,000-3,524,000) / 3,524,000 x 100 = 45%

If we take into account the fact that the rural population rose by 37%, 145/137 - 100 will give us a growth rate per capita of approximately 8%

If we apply our formula 2 we can calculate an average annual growth rate in farming in period 1875-1895:

$g = \Delta \text{ GDP}/n \times 72/100$

$g = 8/20 \times 72/100 = 2/5 \times 72/100 = 144/500 = 0.29\%$

In the literature on the Austro-Hungarian period in Bosnia and Herzegovina, the landless peasants are usually referred to as the serfs (*kmets*). From the Western European point of view this would be a misnomer. In the Western European feudalism serfs were *glede adscriptum* (tied to the land) and could not leave their master. In Bosnia and Herzegovina, the landless peasants were quite mobile. They could have left the land with six month-notice provided they paid their dues to the landowner. Also, the landowner could have evict the peasant and his family if he did not pay his dues. Some landless peasants left the land and joined the industrial workforce although they never lost ties with the village they came from. Those who remained in the village were divided into the two groups; the landless peasants and the small landholders. In both cases the landowners insisted that their plots should have been small so that they could be forced to increase efficiency and productivity. The peasants had to cultivate the land more intensively, and to the extent they managed to do it. Yields per hectare increased by 65% between 1886 and 1904, while the crops increased by 85% in the same period. Production per capita rose by respectable 40%. (Palairet)

If we apply the last formula, we get the following results:

$g = \Delta \text{ GDP}/n \times 72/100$

a) <u>Productivity</u>- $g = 65/18 \times 72/100 = 2.6\%$

b) <u>Crops</u>-g = 85/18 x 72/100 =3.4%
c) <u>Production per head</u> = 40 /18 x 72/100 = 1.6

In spite of this, the overall results in farming were poor. This is easily confirmed if we compare yields in production of wheat, rye, oat, barley, and maize in Bosnia and Herzegovina with the chosen Balkan countries:

Table 2 – Average annual yields in production of various agricultural products in chosen countries 1889-1903

Country	Yields in metric cents	Yield per capita in kilograms
Bosnia and Herzegovina	4,230	245.68
Croatia and Slavonia	10,264	414.57
Serbia	9,752	378.01
Romania	45,942	741.00
Bulgaria	22,655	596.19

SOURCE: Report of the Common Minister of Finance about Administration of Bosnia and Herzegovina, p 222, Zagreb 1906, cited by Kemal Hrelja, op cit. p 149

b) Animal Husbandry

Bosnia and Herzegovina had excellent natural conditions for animal husbandry. Plenty of meadows and pastures, covering one quarter of the territory of the country and the fact that the peasants did not pay the tithe and the third to the state and the landowner created very favorable conditions for this branch of agriculture. The strength of the Bosnian animal husbandry was reflected not only in its quality and fertility, but also in its number. The number of animals, collected by the Austro-Hungarian authorities in 1879, the first year after the occupation, is presented in the following table:

Table 3 – Number of various animals in Bosnia and Herzegovina in 1879

ANIMALS	NUMBER
Horses and donkeys	161,168
Beefs	762,077
Sheep	839,988
Goats	522,123
Pigs	430,354

SOURCE: Landesregierung fur Bosnien und die Hercegovina: Die Landwirtschaft in BiH, p 354-55, table XXVIII, Sarajevo1899, cited by Kemal Hrelja, op. cit, p 7

Although these figures underestimate the number of animals since the peasants gave inaccurate information fearing the cattle requisition, they still show a great wealth of cattle in Bosnia and Herzegovina. With a slightly more than one million inhabitants Bosnia and Herzegovina was one of the richest countries in Europe according to number of cattle per capita. (Hrelja)

In the 1880s the peasants enjoyed virtually unrestricted rights on pastures in forests which at that time mainly belonged to the state. The rise in the value of animals and products was the result of extensive techniques, where low revenue was compensated by the enlargement of the herds. A prevalence of animal husbandry reduced the overall burden which the peasants had to pay to the state and the landowner. (Palairet).

Animal husbandry experienced prosperity until the mid of the 1890s. After that the stagnation followed. A total production increased by a paltry 2% in a period 1887 – 1913. During this period production increased by an average annual growth rate of 0.5%, which was well below an increase in population, which grew at an average annual rate of 1.5%. (Palairet)

There were two factors, one on the supply side, and the other one on the demand side, which contributed to the stagnation in animal husbandry after 1895. On the supply side a fall in the area of pastures by 5% in a period 1886-1904 reduced production, in-spite of the measures undertaken to intensify production. On the demand side a decisive negative influence came from the Hungarians. Bosnia and Hungary competed in agricultural markets and although incorporation in the customs union in 1880 removed tariff barriers, Hungary imposed other obstacles for export of the Bosnian agricultural products into the other parts of the monarchy. Alleged veterinary reasons were usually an excuse for restriction imposed on imports of the Bosnian cattle. In addition, Hungarians banned imports of pigs from Bosnia and Herzegovina and Serbia in 1895 requiring that the pigs first need to be slaughtered. Since Bosnia and Herzegovina did not have the capacities for packing meat the volume of trade fell by 90%. The volume of trade in pigs never recovered, even during the customs war between Serbia and Austro-Hungary in a period 1906-1911. Tax revenue from pig farming tumbled from 141,000 crowns in 1896 to 78,000 crowns in 1902. Although Hungary had some justification in a tighter control of pig imports due to cap and sputum disease, this was not a real reason. Hungarian manipulation with the Bosnian export trade bear part of responsibility for poor performance of the Bosnian agricultural sector. (Palairet)

The following table estimates the overall performance of the agricultural sector in Bosnia and Herzegovina during the entire Austro-Hungarian period:

Table 4 - Bosnia and Herzegovina, sectoral agricultural production

1879 – 1914

(million crowns, prices in 1910)

Year	Animals	Animal products	Marketed crops	Cereals	Vegetables	Total	Total per capita (crowns)
1879	29	25	4	17	2	77	76
1882-1885	43	32	8	28	5	116	105
1886-1890	53	37	12	39	9	150	124
1891-1895	53	36	15	52	13	168	126
1896-1900	61	40	15	49	16	181	126
1901-1905	59	38	14	47	15	174	114
1906-1910	59	37	15	45	19	175	107
1911-1914	61	37	17	60	20	194	113

SOURCE: BALKSTAT, cited by Michael Palairet, op. cit p 249

The table reveals two things, Firstly, agricultural production rose from 1879 until 1895. After that it recorded a negative growth. Secondly, animal husbandry generated the lion's share of agricultural income, ranging from around 70% at the beginning of the period, to more than 85% at the end of the period.

The table also allows us to calculate an average annual growth rate over the entire period. Firstly, we need to calculate the rate of inflation. The average rate of inflation in a period 1870-1896 was -0.86. The average rate of inflation from 1896 until 1914 was 1.36%. For the whole period 1870 – 1914 the average annual rate of inflation was 0.1%. (Gerlach & Stuart).

We can apply our formula (8) to calculate a cumulative inflation over the period 1879 – 1914:

= n x p x 100/72 (8)

= 32 x 0.1 x 100/72 = 4.4%

This means that we need to subtract 4.4% from 113:

(113 x 4.4)/100 = 4.972, rounded off to 5.

Subtracting 5 from 113 we arrive at a figure of 108 crowns per head at prices in 1879.

Now, we can calculate a percentage increase in agricultural production 1879 – 1914:

(108 – 76)/76 x 100 = 42%

If we apply our formula (5)

g = Δ GDP/n x 72/100

we will get g = 42/32 x 72/100 = 0.94%.

If we take into account that even this paltry average annual growth rate might be a good deal the result of better and more efficient data collection in the Austro-Hungarian compared to the Ottoman period we can easily draw a conclusion that majority of rural population saw a little or none improvement in the standard of living.

The following extract describes the quality of life in the Bosnian village: "…….The needs of those workers in villages were minimal and this was most certainly the cheapest workforce in

Europe. ………." *This worker lives the most primitive life. He eats bread, bacon, and black onion; as far as vegetables are concerned, he knows only for beans and cabbage. In that agricultural land a cucumber is a feast, and in-spite of the fact that the country is breeding cattle he eats meat only during religious holidays*" (Hrelja)

TRANSPORT

a) Roads

If one compares the state of the roads in Bosnia and Herzegovina in the early Middle Ages with the state of the roads in the nineteenth century one could easily notice a significant set-back. Bosnia and Herzegovina were covered with a network of intersected roads built by the Romans. While once upon a time these roads transported carts full of goods and people from Dalmatia to rivers Sava, Drina, and Danube, and back, the main transport means in the nineteenth century was the loaded horse. The length of cart roads amounted to 900 KM. Apart from some along the river Sava the main cart road ran from Bosanski Brod in the north to Metkovic in the south, via Sarajevo, Ivan mountain, Konjic and Mostar. This road had a lot of up hills and down hills due to mountainous relief. It did not have ditches and bridges for support, and during torrential rains was flooded and became impassable. (Hrelja)

The Ottoman authorities were aware of a dismal state of roads in the country. In order to improve the roads network they passed "The law on roads" in 1869. The law regulated building, maintenance, and administration of the roads. A primitive subsistence nature of the Bosnian economy envisaged the *corvee* as the main source of labor in building and maintenance of the roads. Predictably, the combination of modern stipulations with the medieval organization of work did not generate any improvements. (Hrelja)

In the 1860s, during the reign of Topal Osman-Pasha, a regular postal service was introduced, as well as a telegraph connecting Sarajevo, Banjaluka and Gradiska on the 17 June 1866. However, these two institutions were badly organized. As a result, they did not contribute much to the improvement in communications. (Hrelja)

The Austro-Hungarians realized the magnitude of the problem related to the lack of adequate transportation facilities when their army marched into the country. This is why for both military and economic reasons transportation became the first priority of the new administration. In the first few years of the Austro-Hungarian rule the road construction was of the greatest importance. The budget and the special reports issued by the *Landesregierung* have shown that in 1880 Bosnia and Herzegovina had a total of 1,542.81 kilometers of roads. But the reports did not show the length of roads built by the army of occupation nor does it mention the classification of roads. The maintenance of these roads required 60,400 florins and 534,711 days of corvee valued at 795,125 florins. While these amounts were spent on existing roads, 81.3 kilometers of first-class roads (*Hauptstrassen)*and 115.9 kilometers of second-class roads (*Bezirksstrassen)*and 60 kilometers of third-class roads (*Gemeindestrassen)* were under construction in 1881. These figures show that the volume of construction activity was considerable, and also that the budget figures on road building expenditure covered only the cost of materials and the salaries of qualified work force such as engineers, foremen, and other specialists. Labor was supplied by the peasantry's *corvee* obligations without payment. The *corvee* system, anachronic as it was, had to be used in a view of limited financial resources of the *Landesregierung.* (Sugar)

The fact that military and economic needs were not identical prompted the authorities to schedule a ten-year construction plan. This program, together with a financial plan was submitted to the Ministry of Finance. The program envisaged total expenditures of 3,336,000 florins. The cost of building first-class roads, were estimated at 450,000 florins a year for the five years, with additional 200,000 florins needed for maintenance. According to the program all first-class roads were to be finished by the end of 1889, and the entire road network by the end of 1893. The program was adopted and by the end of 1891 the length of roads built after the occupation began amounted to 1,965 kilometers. (Sugar)

The cash spent on the roads totaled 6% of the government's income, amounting 10,187,650 florins, out of which 19.5%, or 2,100,000 florins accounted for the value of the *corvee*. It is clear that the corvee made a significant contribution to the development of roads network in Bosnia and Herzegovina. The program was a successful compromise of various views and needs, and gave the country a well-planned road network which served military and economic requirements equally well. (Sugar)

b) Railways

The only railway built before the occupation was the one which connected Banjaluka and Dobrljin, amounting 104.33 kilometers. The plan for the Ostban (The Oriental railway) was designed by baron Hirsch, and executed by the "COMPAGNIE GENERALE POUR EXPLOATATION DES CHEMINE DE FER DE LA TURQUE D'EUROPE (The General Company for exploitation of the railways of the European Turkey). This branch was built in the northern-western part of the country and did not contribute at all to the improvement in communications in Bosnia. The railway ceased to operate after the Great Uprising in 1875 and all the fleet was deposited at Banjaluka. (Hrelja)

The Austro-Hungarian authorities were aware that their priority was to build the railway infrastructure in Bosnia and Herzegovina. However, unlike building the roads, there was no plan to build the railway network. The various lines were built piecemeal. The interests of Bosnia and Herzegovina and general economic consideration were not taken into account when the representatives of the various Austrian and Hungarian pressure groups discussed the lines of the country's railway. In addition, the *Landesregierung* and *Kreisleiter* who represented the country's interests when the program was established, were never involved in the discussion relevant to the building of the railway network. This is in-spite of the fact that works on the railway infrastructure were partly financed by the taxes collected in the country. (Sugar)

There were two types of frictions which impeded a smooth development of the railway network; the conflict between strategic/political, military and economic aims, and the conflict between the interests of the Austrians and the interests of the Hungarians.

One of the main forces behind the railway program was the army. It held the management of the Banjaluka-Dobrljin railway, which represented the shortest route leading towards Austria. During the war operations the army built the Bosanski Brod- Zenica line to facilitate logistic support. Also, the army insisted that the track be extended first to Sarajevo and then to Mostar, the two main garrison cities of the country. Building this line was also justified from the economic point of view. It connected the country's two capital cities, Sarajevo and Mostar, and main economic centers with the rest of the Monarchy. But the Gabela-Zelenika, Hum-Trebinje and Uskoplja-Gravosa sectors of the railway, which always operated at a loss, had only military value. (Sugar)

In other cases political considerations were stronger compared to military and economic factors together. The best example of this political pressure is the history of the Bugojno-Arzano and the Banjaluka-Jajce-Bugojno lines. The military wanted them because they would have connected Split, an important military port, with the main line of the country and would also have created a link between the Bosanski Brod-Mostar and the Banjaluka-Dobrljin railways, enabling fast troop movements from Austrian garrisons to the center of the country. (Sugar)

Frictions between the Austrians and the Hungarians is best illustrated in disputes related to the building of the aforementioned railway. The Austrians were vitally interested in connecting Dalmatia with the rest of Austria, so that they have better access for their goods to the Bosnian market. For this reason the Hungarians always prevented the construction of the aforementioned railways. The Bugojno-Arzano line alone would have connected Sarajevo with Trieste via the port of Split. This would have reduced the transport costs for the Austrian firms compared to the Vienna-Budapest-Szeged-Bosanski Brod-Sarajevo route. In addition, this route would have increased the competition to the Hungarian industry and cut into the revenue of the Hungarian railways, which charged high fares for the shipment of Austrian goods. The Hungarians also did not want competition to their only sea port in Fiume, which being the shortest distance from Sarajevo by rail, handled most of the country's export trade. Once the Ostbahn had been completed, the Hungarian resistance grew even stronger, as this same line could have channeled much of the Serbian export trade, going mainly through Hungary, to Split. As the Banjaluka-Jajce railway would have given the advantage of a shorter route for Austrian products shipped to Bosnia and Herzegovina, the Hungarians opposed this line as well. The Austrians retaliated by opposing and preventing the building of the Samac-Doboj and Brcko-Celic-Bjelina-Raca railway desperately needed by the economically most important part of the country, the Posavina, because they would have run through northeastern Bosnia, and thus would have belonged to the Hungarian railways. (Sugar)

Additional problem was how to raise the money for the project. Tax revenue did not provide sufficient funds, so the obvious solution was to obtain a loan. Kallay approached the Rothschild bank and the Union bank, but he was turned down. Then, he pulled some strings and applied for the loan in the Wiener Bankverein, where his brother-in-law Count Bethlen, and count Tisza's brother had interest and influence. In order to win over the military Kallay planned to allocate a portion of the loan for extension, repairment and maintenance of barracks.

Kallay had to obtain the backing of the two Parliaments. The two Parliaments approved of his plan when he promised to use a portion of the loan to pay off the entire debt owed to the Common Credit for the first two loans granted for the railways in Bosnia and Herzegovina. Kallay needed 4.7 million florins, out of which 3.5 million for repairs of the existing lines, and 1.2 million florins for unforeseen expenses on the Lasva-Bugojno-Donji Vakuf-Jajce railway under construction. In order to obtain permission to secure the money he needed , Kallay made the following proposition: new investment on existing lines of 3.5 million florins, new barracks for the army 2 million florins, and repayment of the first two Common Credit for 4.4 million florins, the Lasva-Bugojno-Donji Vakuf railway for 1.2 million florins for a total of 11,298,461.82 florins, deducting 1894 payments to Common Credits of 160,000 florins and adding financing charges of 861,538.18 florins would leave a balance of expenditures of 12,000,000 florins. (Sugar)

This plan was accepted by both governments and Parliaments, and Francis Joseph signed the authorization on July 8, 1895. The loan was secured by bonds issued by the *Landesregierung*. The bonds paid 4% interest, and were redeemable after sixty years. The *Wienerbankverein* agreed to advance the money and to place the bonds for the financing charge and for the right to establish a branch in Bosnia and Herzegovina under the name of *Privilegierte Landesbank* fur *Bosnien und die Hercegovina*. The first word in the bank's name meant that it was to be the exclusive fiscal agent of the *Landesregierung*. (Sugar)

More than 90% of railways was a narrow gauge. The narrow gauge was cheaper and quicker to build. A decision to build a narrow gauge was logical in the country which desperately needed the railway network for its economic development. However, as the economy grew, the narrow gauge proved to be inadequate. An alternative strategy to build the standard gauge would have been a significant drain of the resources of a poor country.

The railway network was supposed to be profitable. However, the railways which Bosnia and Herzegovina acquired were always on the infusion. Although the first two loans granted to Bosnia and Herzegovina from the Common Credits were repaid, the country still owed central finances 16,200,000 florins on the above amount. Tardy or defaulted payments, with their extra interests, brought the total debt to this extremely high amount. The railways were not able to produce necessary revenues.

The only profitable railway line was Bosanski Brod- Sarajevo. In some years this line was able to make a profit which would offset losses on the other lines. However, the revenue of the railways was never enough to cover amortization, interests, necessary repairs, and the purchase of needed rolling stock. (Sugar)

The rolling stock increased by 96% from 1900 to 1909. If we apply our formula:

$g = \Delta\ GDP \times 72/n \times 100$

we will arrive at $g = 96 \times 72/9 \times 100$, or an average growth rate of 7.68%, which is a respectable figure. However, the volume of transport measured by tons-kilometers increased by 120% in the same period. The same formula will give us

$g = 120 \times 72/9 \times 100$ an average growth rate of 9.6%.

By 1909 the rolling stock became a bottleneck of the Bosnian railway system As a result the supply of raw materials was very often delayed, causing stoppages in the industrial production. Commercial and industrial companies were forced to pay workers who remained idle because of lack of the rolling stock. All this was the result of the discrepancy between the volume of trade and the amount of the rolling stock. (Hrelja)

The total length of railways amounted to 1517 kilometers, out of which 999 kilometers were owned by the state, and the remaining 518 kilometers were privately owned forest railways. The problem was conceptual. If the railways were mainly owned by the state then they should have been treated as a public utility; If the aim was to make them profitable then they should have been given to the private sector.

In order to make railways profitable the tariff rates were set very high. "For the distance from Bosanski Brod-Sarajevo in florins per 100 kilograms for carload quantities, the rates were as follows: by rail and wagon, 6.99 for food, 9.75 for general merchandise; by wagon alone, 6.50 for food, 7.50 for general merchandise. In 1880 rates in kreuzers for 100 kilograms per kilometer compared to those of the Austrian railroads as follows: Bosnia-Herzegovina, 1.50 for food, 2.50 for animals and other goods; Austria, 0.42 for food, 0.62 for animals and other goods. Although experts pointed out in the Delegations that the railroad would never capture the trade of the ships and wagons unless they brought their rates down to the level of those charged in Austria-Hungary, the tariff policy in Bosnia and Herzegovina did not change. In 1913 the rates in heller per 100 kilograms for general merchandise in carload quantities of the Bosnia-Herzegovinian railroads compared with those in Hungary as follows: 50 kilometers, 43 and 26; 100 kilometers, 73 and 45; 200 kilometers, 143 and 81; and 300 kilometers, 206 and 109. This freight policy was detrimental not only to the profitability of the railroads, but also created difficulties for those of Bosnia-Herzegovina's industries which depended on export markets for their sales". (Sugar)

The financial failure of the railways was not the fault of the management. Two other factors were responsible; the economic one, and the fiscal one. Economic considerations were a great deal neglected when the lines were planned. As a result a network was built in the regions where the economy could not support the railways. In addition, the railways should have paid for themselves and should have also produce a surplus for the government. Those who were in charge of the freight policy set overly high tariffs, overlooking the price elasticity of demand and the fact that they deteriorated the competitiveness of the Bosnian exporting companies in foreign markets.

In-spite of these failures, the country's railway system efficiently operated and the capital invested in them was obtained through long-term and relatively cheap loans. The efficiency of the system, notwithstanding some technical mistakes committed by its builders, was secured by the foreign experts. The trains ran on time in any weather with a speed of 30 kilometers per hour. The freight cars were able to carry 10 metric tons each, and freight trains could handle as many as twenty-five of these cars. Nobody ever had any objections on the way in which the railways were run in Bosnia and Herzegovina. (Sugar)

Although the railway system did not contribute to the economic development of the country as it should have, and although it became obsolete, and in need of reconstruction around the beginning of the WWI, one must be impressed with the fact that the railway network increased by a staggering 13 times in 36 years. In addition, for the sake of mitigating the criticism of the railway policy, one must admit that there were plans to build lines with a standard gauge in which Bosnia and Herzegovina would participate with one third and Austria-Hungary with two thirds finances. However, the plans were disrupted by the war. (Juzbasic)

TRADE AND MONEY

a) Trade

Before the occupation trade and money economy were rudimentary. In the country in which more than 90% of population were employed in agriculture a subsistence economy prevailed. The peasants produced everything what they needed for their modest standard of living; food, tools, simple equipment, clothes, and even houses. They were in possession of money twice a year; in autumn, after they sold their crops, and in spring, after they sold cattle. Even then they would retain money rarely since they had to pay off loans and merchandise credits. A good deal of trade between the peasants took the form of a barter trade in which goods were exchanged without the use of money. (Hrelja)

Apart from occasional fairs, one transitory form of trade existed between the village and the town. A surplus of home-made products was sold either directly or through the middleman to the urban merchants. Hardworking women generated a massive surplus of carpets, embroidery and similar products, which were traded for iron tools and various household gadgets. (Schmid)

Foreign trade was more developed than internal trade. Naturally, the bulk was oriented towards the Orient, although in the last decades of the Ottoman rule there was an influx of modern manufacturing products from the West. In 1865 the country recorded a small surplus in trade balance. The main exporting articles were cattle, corn, leather and related products, sheep wool, plums, iron, wine, tobacco and wood. Imports was dominated by a colonial goods such as sugar, cotton, silk, textiles, and final products of wool. Luxury products such as corrals, clothes, weapons were imported. Foreign trade was impeded by an overall insecurity and poor communications caused by a lack of railways and low quality roads in which draft horses still prevailed as the main transport means. (Schmid)

After the occupation the volume of trade rose manifold. The influx of soldiers, administrative personnel and experts in various fields significantly increased demand for all sorts of goods and services. The Sephardic Jews, who were dominant in trade in the Ottoman period, were now joined by the Ashkenazi Jews, who arrived from all parts of the Austro-Hungarian Monarchy and permanently settled in Bosnia and Herzegovina. Also, the Serbs increased their participation in trade. There were many prominent Serb merchants even before the occupation and they dominated the foreign trade. With increased demand for many goods and services some Serbs switched from crafts to commerce looking for more lucrative source of profit. (Hauptmann)

Before the occupation Sarajevo was a commercial center of the country. After the occupation the central role of Sarajevo in trade was temporarily endangered. Two factors contributed to this. Firstly, many previously isolated places had been connected by roads and railways and they did not need to purchase goods via Sarajevo since they could now do it directly. Secondly, the move of a tariff border to the southeast, after Bosnia and Herzegovina was incorporated into a common customs union in 1880 increased the significance of the Salonika market at the expense of the Sarajevo market. Even Austro-Hungarian garrisons in Bijelo Polje, Pljevlje, and Prijepolje got their supplies in Salonika. (Hauptmann)

The following table can give as indirect information about a pace with which the volume of trade grew after the occupation:

Table 5 - A revenue from indirect taxes in Bosnia and Herzegovina

1885 – 1913 in crowns

YEAR	INDIRECT TAXES
1885	6,226,837
1890	12,817,983
1895	16,011,791
1900	18,713,529
1905	22,791,856
1910	32,788,753
1913	43,429,483

SOURCE: Adapted from Ferdinand Hauptmann: "Austrougarska vladavina u Bosni i Hercegovini 1878-1918", p 129 (The Austro-Hungarian administration in Bosnia and Herzegovina 1878-1918), in Enver Redzic (editor): "Prilozi za istoriju Bosne i Hercegovine", (Contributions for the History of Bosnia and Herzegovina), ANUBiH, Sarajevo 2006

Indirect taxes mainly consisted of monopolies, sales tax, and excise duties. Their sharp increase reflects a vigorous rise in purchasing power of population, and consequently a rise in the volume of trade.

We can use our formula (5) to calculate a growth rate of trade for each and every period.

$g = (72 \times \Delta GDP)/100 \times n$

1885-1890;

$\Delta GDP = (12.8 - 6.2)/6.2 \times 100 = 3,300 : 31 = 106\%$

$g = (106 \times 72) / (100 \times 5) = 7632 : 500 = 15.4\%$

1890 – 1895;

$\Delta GDP = (16 - 12.8)/12.8 \times 100 = 320 : 12.8 = 40\%$

$g = (72 \times 40) /500 = 5.76\%$

1895 – 1900;

$\Delta GDP = (18.7 - 16) /16 \times 100 = 2700:16 = 17\%$

$g = (72 \times 17) / 500 = 2.45\%$

1900 – 1905;

$\Delta GDP = (22.8 - 18.7) /18.7 \times 100 = 410:18.7 = 22\%$

$g = (72 \times 22) / 500 = 3.17\%$

1905 – 1910;

Δ GDP = (32.8 – 22.8) /22.8 x 100 = 1,000: 22.8 = 44%

g = (72 x 44) / 500 = 6.34%

1910 – 1913;

Δ GDP = (43.4 – 32.8) / 32.8 x 100 = 1060:328 = 32.3%

g= (72 x 32) / 100 x 3 = 7.75%

Starting from low levels, indirect taxes rose by a staggering 15.4 % per annum from 1885 until 1890. In the following two five-year periods a rate of growth of purchasing power was sharply reduced, but in the eight years before the war the rate of growth recuperated, probably reflecting industrial expansion, followed by urbanization, and absorption of pockets of previously subsistence economy into a market economy.

For the whole period 1885 – 1913 indirect taxes increased seven-fold.

We can use our formula for a seven-fold increase in a variable to calculate the average annual growth rate of purchasing power:

g = 198 /n; g = 198 / 28 = 7.1%[5]

Expansion of trade led to more intensive links between the merchants and the establishment of their professional

---

[5] This figure is a good indicator of a rise in consumption, which is by far the largest component of the aggregate demand. In modern economies consumption normally accounts for 60-65% of the total aggregate demand. In the analyzed period government expenditures absorbed much lower proportion of the aggregate demand compared to modern economies. This means that at that time consumption accounted for even a higher percentage of income. This is the reason why a calculated growth rate of consumption is a fairly good indicator of the pace of growth of non-agricultural sectors of the Bosnian economy.

organizations. Economic and Trade Chamber was created in Sarajevo. In 1906 the General Merchants' Union with more than 200 members was established. In addition, many specialist merchants' unions were created. One of these, The *Kreditreform*, was formed in 1903 in Sarajevo. (Schmid)

Many semi-official and private merchants' societies were created with the aim of strengthening the relationship between the Monarchies and the Bosnian merchants' institutions. The Hungarian and the Austrian trade museums were established. Their aim was to promote the relationship between the Bosnian and the merchants from the two parts of the Monarchy. The Austrian merchant museum opened its branch in March 1912 in Sarajevo. In this way negotiations and common interests were promoted between the Bosnian merchants and the merchants from the two parts of the Empire. In Austria "the Austrian-Bosnian-Herzegovinian interest society was created in 1911, while in Hungary "the Hungarian -Bosnian-Herzegovinian Economic Central Office" was opened in 1912. Both the institutions were taken care of in the Trade Chambers in Vienna and Budapest. (Schmid)

In 1878 the value of foreign trade of Bosnia and Herzegovina amounted to 36 million crowns (exports 20 million, imports 16 million). The main foreign trade partner was the Austro-Hungarian Monarchy. More than 80% of this trade went via Trieste and Vienna, and the bulk of foreign trade was conducted by the Serb merchants. (Juzbasic)

From the occupation until 1912 the volume of foreign trade rose by almost nine times, to amount to 305 million crowns (exports 130 million, imports 174 million). This was the result of two factors; incorporation of Bosnia and Herzegovina into a common customs union in 1880, and economic expansion, which enormously increased the purchasing power of domestic economic agents. This was reflected in the value of exports, which increased by almost eleven times.

We can use our formula to calculate the average growth rate of foreign trade in a period 1878-1912:

$$(\Delta Y + Y)/Y = (1 + g)^n$$

$$9 = (1 + g)^n$$

We need firstly to discount the number 9 with the factor 1.044, to allow for inflation.

$$8.62 = (1 + g)^n /\log$$

$$\log 8.62 = n \log (1 + g)^n$$

$$0.9355 = 35 \log (1 + g)$$

$$\log (1 + g) = 0.9355/35$$

$$\log (1 + g) = 0.0267$$

$$(1 + g) = 10^{0.0267}$$
$$(1 + g) = 1.0634$$

$$g = 1.0634 - 1$$

$$g = 0.0634$$

$$g = 6.34\%$$

Foreign trade grew at an average annual growth rate of 6.34% in a period 1878-1912.

With the exception of period 1904-1906, the trade balance was in deficit. This was the result of volatility of the prices of agricultural products and an increase in prices of finished goods, particularly machinery and equipment imported from Austria.

However, a balance of payments was not in deficit due to what in vocabulary of a modern balance of payments theory would be dubbed unilateral transfers. Since part of imports consisted of military goods it was paid by the Austrians. (Juzbasic)

The structure of the Bosnian foreign trade shows the features of an underdeveloped economy, in which 83% of exports consisted of raw materials. Wood products were the most important exporting items. Unlike other goods only one quarter of their exports went to the Austro-Hungarian Monarchy. Semi-finished products of wood industry prevailed, while furniture and other final products were imported. Apart from wood and coal, agricultural products were important exporting staples. The leading agricultural exporting articles were heads of cattle, whose exports averaged 200,000-300,000 a year, and plums, with an average exports of 800 wagons a year. Pig iron, iron wares, and chemical products were also very important exporting items. Unlike exports, two thirds of imports consisted of finished products. The main importing staples were cereals, lenses, rice, flour, drinks, textile industry products, and finished products of some other industrial branches. A volume of exports was three times greater than a volume of imports, but the value of imports was greater than the value of exports. This was the result of backwardness of agriculture and unfavorable structure of the Bosnian industry in which extractive industry for exports prevailed. (Juzbasic)

b) Money

Before the occupation, the use of money was quite limited in a predominantly subsistence economy. Exchange mainly took a form of a barter trade and money was used only to settle the differences. In addition, money had less a function of a medium of exchange and more assumed functions of the unit of account and the store of value. (Schmid)

The main currency was the Turkish piaster (grosz). Also, there was a golden coin, the mejejidi, worth 100 piasters, and silver the jimirkili, worth 20 piasters. In addition, there was English, French, and Italian money in circulation. (Hauptmann)

In 1876 the Ottoman government issued paper money the *kaime,* whose value was rapidly falling. The Ottoman government forced merchants to accept it with a threat of punishment, but they tried to get rid of it as soon as possible and kept gold coins as the hoard.

After the occupation, the Austro-Hungarian authorities tried to regulate the money circulation. They immediately banned the use of the *kaime*, and wanted to reduce the circulation of the Turkish gold and silver money. Since they were obliged to use the Turkish money they employed it only in trade with the Ottoman empire, and the rest sent to Vienna where it was replaced by the various types of the Austro-Hungarian money.

Parallel with a gradual replacement of the Turkish money went a trend of an increasing use of banknotes instead of coinage. According to one tender of the government in 1879 all payments to the military must be conducted with at least 80% of banknotes. In other words, the authorities wanted to secure the circulation of banknotes in Bosnia and Herzegovina so that they would not be squeezed out by the coinage. The main aim of coinage withdrawal and its replacement with banknotes was to improve the liquidity of the Bosnian economy and supply the Bosnian market with enough funds for its expected growth. (Hauptmann)

Although expected growth of market materialized it, did not contribute to economic development. The money earned by domestic producers and merchants was not used for repeated purchases and investments but was rather hoarded. For a long period of time individuals had to hide surpluses of money and were not ready to inject it into a whirl of uncertain earnings and speculation. Therefore, surpluses of money did not help entrepreneurs but enhanced the inherited tendency of rentierism. In such a situation, foreigners of a dodgy provenance filled in the gap, rushing into Bosnia and Herzegovina with a prospect of earning "a quick buck". Only after the monetary situation stabilized and after it was clear that the Austro-Hungarian presence in the country will not be temporary, money started getting its more productive employment. (Hauptmann)

CREDIT, FINANCIAL INSTITUTIONS AND CAPITAL

a) Credit

Before the occupation in a predominantly subsistence economy credit and financial institutions were poorly developed. The only "financial institution" was *Menafi-Sanduks*, a sort of aid fund, where certain percentage of tenth would be stored in barns as an emergency supply, and later sold. Finances were in hands of the members of the county council. A lion's share of the finance from this fund were owned by the officials. As a result, wealthy citizens reaped the benefits from these funds, not wider layers of population.

The Ottoman authorities tried to introduce some kind of compulsory aid funds in the 1860s. This attempt produced poor results in Bosnia. Borrowers, mainly the peasants, were charged astronomic interest which they were not able to repay. In addition, administration and registration were so poor, that most of transactions were not recorded. As a result, these funds were depleted. (Schmid).

Mortgages were almost non-existent. The Ottoman system did not recognize the use of immovable property as a collateral. The only known collateral were crops. In such a situation borrowers had to turn to the private lenders.

The private lenders were mainly merchants, most of them Serbs and Sephardic Jews. They charged exorbitant interest rates which sometimes amounted to 100% per annum, although the maximum permitted interest rate by the law was 12%. Sometimes, the usurers were not merchants, in which case they acted as intermediaries between the merchants and the peasants. There was usually a friendly relationship between the merchants and the usurers, both of them exploiting illiteracy and ignorance of the peasants to charge them higher prices for colonial and other goods, and at the same time ripping them off by calculating exorbitant interest rates for the credit the latter needed to purchase these goods.

The urban population had a better deal compared to the peasants. They normally paid 18% interest for a trade credit, while property owners had to pay interest at the rate of 24%. (Schmid)

The occupation of Bosnia and Herzegovina brought profound changes in socio-economic relations. The influx of soldiers, administrative workers, civil servants, merchants and settlers from all parts of the monarchy significantly increased the amount of money in circulation. As a result, the level of prices and demand for money rose considerably. The peasants were sucked up in monetary transactions, and there tenth in kind turned into a monetary tenth. Villages, which were dormant in a medieval tranquility for centuries were drawn into a monetized economy. (Schmid)

Such deep breakthrough was also reflected in a need for different organization of credit. The peasants had increased need for credit. Since most of them did not own their land and houses, they had to turn to the usurers, whose role became indispensable, and to cash boxes, usually in the hands of the merchants.

But there was another layer of population, namely the urban dwellers, which were in need for credit organization. This part of population comprised not only craftsmen and merchants, but also wider layers of urban dwellers, which stood in between landowners and merchants, and which included property speculators. The new regulation included land registry, which gave a boost to the emergence of mortgage transactions. The land law, enacted in 1884 forbade the right of repurchase of deposits. Likewise, the new law provided for the legal clarification of the properties under *Kmetenband* and regulated the right of subrogation in a way that corresponded more to economic interests. The law also laid the grounds for a sharp increase in the demand for a real estate landing. (Schmid)

In 1883 an agreement with the Wiener Union Bank was struck with a view of developing mortgage market. The bank assumed responsibility of providing various services and assuring mortgages to businesses with the obligation to expand mortgage markets in official way. The aim the land government had in mind was the enhancement of credit capability of businesses including those who were not included in contracts and conducting these transactions and activities through official channels such as tax office.

This activity was accompanied by attempts to sort out land and property register in every district. A required deposit for mortgages was 50%. A precondition for getting mortgages was assurance that buildings were built from solid material, and that they were fire proof. Mortgages were normally provided with 6% interest rate and repayment period was ten years. In 1886 it was stipulated that the *WienerUnionBank* had the privilege of collecting debts which were applicable also when the government concluded contracts with official pension fund. In this way a failure to honor payment obligation was treated in the same way as tax evasion. (Schmid)

In 1889 the Official Pension Fund was detached from provision of mortgages and a separate Bosnian- Herzegovinian Mortgage Institution was established. This institution was entitled to issue bonds amounting twenty times of the Guarantee fund. The new institution inherited a right of compulsory collection of accumulated debts. The previous regulation was valid for the new institution with the only one minor modification. The repayment period was extended to 10-20 years and the interest rate was slightly reduced to 5.5%. In the case of serfs, transfers debts were alleviated by the possibility to pay them of in different ways with interest rate being reduced to 3%. The institution disposed with the sum of 200,000 crowns. (Schmid)

Hand in hand with the organization of mortgages went activities in organizing personal credit. The law on usury was passed with the aim of curbing rapacious loan sharks' transactions. The authorities were aware that such a widespread lending with exorbitant interest rates was a serious impediment to normal economic life. In order to help the rural population aid funds were established. They got the name "support funds". The government encouraged local population to put money in these funds in the form of interest-bearing deposits. The first such institution was created in a district of Gacko in Eastern Herzegovina in 1886 where the peasants were in a desperate need for money. (Schmid)

Two other funds were established, namely the reserve fund and the support fund in order to provide necessary funds for desperate rural population. The peasants, who took a loan, could have pay it off either in money with interest, or in kind. Any unspent money, in these funds could have been invested profitably, if it did not exceed one third of accumulated interest.

There were two class of loans, the Class A, and the Class B. The first class loan was aimed at financing life provisions, paying off usury loans, purchasing seeds, fodder, working cattle and agricultural tools. The class B loans did not have a particular aim, but had a general purpose of improving and increasing the working cattle, reclamation of land, improving accommodation and agricultural buildings or purchasing land for the sake of their rounding off. The purpose of the class A was taxative, while the purpose of the class B loans was demonstrative. The maximum amount of the class A loan was 200 crowns and the interest rate was 4%. The interest rate on the class B loans matched the government one and was 6%. The loan could be given either in money or in kind. The loan was supposed to be returned at once, but in more difficult circumstances paying of in instalments was permitted. The repayment term was not supposed to exceed one year. The reserve fund was used only for the class A loans. These funds had the special statute which regulated its activities. There were 51 such funds in 1906 in Bosnia and Herzegovina. (Schmid)

Parallel with sorting out the credit for the rural population the government undertook activities of organizing credit for business people, merchants, and the urban population. From 1900 the support funds were established for merchants and business people. The resources of these funds were provided by a combination of voluntary contributions of participants and part given by the government. All participants were obliged to deposit at least 12 crowns per annum in the fund either upfront or in instalments. The interest rate did not exceed 4%. The participants were allowed to capitalize their deposits if they did not exceed 400 crowns. The loans were short-term and had to be repaid by the end of the term. For loans which exceeded 400 crowns, special permission and a guarantee of two witnesses was required. It was stipulated that interest rate for these loans should not be higher than 6%. These funds were managed by district representatives, and in Sarajevo by the government commissioner. The reserve fund and security deposits, which accompanied these funds were mandatory. In 1906 there were 4 of these funds created in Sarajevo, Travnik, Prijedor, and Foca. The number increased to 8 in 1911. (Schmid)

b) Capital

The law forbade the use of the monarchy's finances in Bosnia and Herzegovina. In addition, foreign capital was not keen to invest in such a backward country with poor infrastructure. In such a situation the government had to take care about provision of finances for economic development and its budget. Unresolved socio-economic relations in agriculture excluded this industry as a source of capital. The government had to turn to forestry where Bosnia and Herzegovina had an enormous wealth of resources.

Immediately after the occupation, the Austro-Hungarian authorities had started sending experts whose task was to estimate the forest wealth. Their findings were positive as regards forest and ore wealth. A difficult access and a lack of appropriate infrastructure reduced the value of this wealth. Inspite of this the authorities seize the opportunity to exploit this natural resource and use it as a source of capital.

Austrian experts recommended cutting of oak trees. This product was demanded in foreign markets and did not require sophisticated technology or investment in transport infrastructure. In addition, a sale of oak trees provided revenue for the government. Through tenders, direct deals with individual buyers and auctions the government managed to sell 144,000 oak trees with 288,000 cubic meters of wood until 1885. From 1886 the government changed the system of sale by signing long-term contracts with certain buyers, with required deposits. This arrangement was mutually beneficial. The government could be sure that this activity would bring a fixed and certain amount of revenue, while entrepreneurs were protected from price fluctuations since the price was fixed and low. One of the first companies involved in these contracts was the "Morpurgo and Parente" firm from Trieste, which alone cut 1,300,000 oak trees with the mass of 2,600,000 cubic meters of wood. (Hauptmann)

Foreign capital was very cautious in the years immediately after the occupation. The government had to offer significant privileges to foreign financial institutions in order to raise their interest in investing in Bosnia and Herzegovina. In 1883 the government managed to attract the Wiener Union Bank to established its branch in Sarajevo with a capital of 2,000,000 forints. The bank received great privileges; a right to conduct business transactions with immovable property, a right to do transactions with industrial, mining, and agricultural products; a possibility to establish its own companies, and a right to perform all monetary transactions for the government with only obligation to pay taxes. In 1884 the bank got the right to sell tobacco and did this lucrative job until 1998, although the administration reduced the bank's profit from 6% to 5,5%, and later to 4%. The bank remained the sole monetary institution for many years and helped the implementation of the country's industrial policy. The government obtained a loan amounting 500,000 florins in 1892, and 1,200,000 florins in 1985. The government used this money to undertake activities in the above- mentioned industrial sectors of the economy. (Hauptmann)

c) Financial institutions

For many years the Wiener Union Bank was the only foreign financial institution in Bosnia and Herzegovina. Involvement of the banking sector in the Bosnian economy expanded in the second part of the 1880s. The *Bodencreditanstalt* from Vienna financed works on Doboj-Simin han railway in 1895 since the Wiener Union Bank was not interested in the project. In the same years a combined capital of the *Wiener Bankverein* and the Hungarian bank helped the establishment of the Landbank with the capital of 8,000,000 crowns. The Landbank was a privileged bank and played a function of the Central bank in Bosnia and Herzegovina. (Hauptmann)

The Landbank took over mortgage transactions with a right to issue bonds in the amount thirty times greater than the capital which was paid in. The Landbank had a privilege of enforcing payment immediately and was allowed to issue certificates for free. The security fund was established to ensure the capital for bonds, and the money from repaid mortgages was denied the function of a redemption fund. The interest rate on bonds was fixed by the government at 5 pre cent. (Schmid).

Behind the Landbank the mortgage transactions expanded to involve some domestic and 14 foreign credit institutions. The biggest foreign credit institutions involved in mortgage transactions in 1909 were *die Laibacher Kredit bank* (354,000 crowns), *die Serbische Bank in Budapest* (200,000 crowns), die

Szabadkaer Sparkasse (200,000 crowns), *der allgemeine Grazer Selbst-hilferein* (102,200 crowns), *die Serbische Bank in Agram* (90,716 crowns), *die Serbische Kreditbank in Brod* (75,316 crowns), and *die Erste kroatische Sparkasse in Agram* (61,373 crowns).

In the last years before WWI, big mortgage credit institutions in the empire started to increase their attention to Bosnia and Herzegovina. Two credit institutions, namely *Bodenkreditanstalt,* and the *Unionbank* merged under the name "*Osterreichisch-bosnische Bank*". The new institution was located in Sarajevo and its main activities were related to mortgages. The new institution started its operations in 1912.

A total value of mortgages was 1,874,376 crowns in 1893. It increased to 77,420,670 crowns in 1904, and to 114,832,244 crowns in 1909. For the last years before the WWI the evidence is unfortunately missing. (Schmid)

Before the WWII there were four banks from the Monarchy, with a combined capital of 88 million crowns. At the same time there were 50 domestic institutions (banks, saving houses) with a total capital of 43.1 million crowns. The first domestic financial institution was established in a town of Brcko in 1889. Brcko was a major exporting center for Bosnian products such as plums and pigs. As a result, there were many merchants in the town, who were supported by the authorities to open the first saving house. Banjaluka and Bijeljina followed the example of Brcko and opened similar saving houses. The government efforts to mobilize domestic capital and put it in a productive employment produced visible results when in 1906 the Brcko saving house merged with the *Landbank in Sarajevo.* (Hauptmann)

Merchants from Brcko put 50,000-70,000 florins (1 florin = 0.50 crowns) in a guarantee fund, and took an obligation of a further 20,000 florins. Merchant-entrepreneur layer in Brcko, which established the first saving house, was the most advanced and a role model for the rest of the country. It was multiethnic in its composition, including Serbs, Muslims, Jews, and Germans. All other domestic financial institutions, however, were organized on an ethnic base. The biggest ones were the Serb Central Bank, established in 1911, with a capital of 3 million crowns, the Croatian Central Bank, established in 1907, with a capital of 2 million crowns, and the Muslim Central Bank, established in 1911, with a capital of 3 million crowns. These financial institutions were incorporated in a wider banking network of the Monarchy (Zagreb, Ljubljana, Prague). They laid the grounds of ethnic-political formation. The special role in this network was given to the institution of agricultural credit cooperatives. There were 192 such cooperatives in 1913. Serb cooperatives were the most numerous (113), followed by the Croatian ones (64). German colonists had 10, Muslims 4, and Ukrainian colonists 1 cooperative. In financial terms the strongest were the Croatian cooperatives, outpacing the Serb cooperatives in a ratio 6 to 1. (Hauptmann)

In a relatively short period of time the administration managed to replace the subsistence economy with a dense network of credit institutions. However, domestic capital was insufficient for big investment projects. Its role in modernization of the agrarian society of Bosnia and Herzegovina was therefore modest. A side effect of undercapitalization of domestic financial institutions was reliance of the peasants on usurers. In 1912/14 loans issued by individuals amounted to 42%. (Hauptmann)

MINING

a) Coal Mining

The first mine of brown coal in Bosnia and Herzegovina was opened in Zenica. The state started exploitation in 1880. This mine was the first industrial enterprise in the country. The thickness of coal layer was around 10 meters and caloric value ranged from 4,800 to 5,000. The mine had a favorable location since it was situated near the railway Sarajevo-Bosanski Brod. Good location and richness of the coal layers inspired the government to invest huge funds in technical equipment.

Apart from this mine the most important pits were opened in Kakanj, Kreka, Breza, Banja Luka and Una D.D. near Dobrljina. (Hrelja).

The largest number of mines was owned by the state. Out of 19 mines, 4 were privately owned, three were rented to the private owners, and 2 were organized as limited companies. The remaining 10 mines were in state ownership. Monopolistic character of mining was even more pronounced when figures on production are applied:

Table 6 - Production of coal in Bosnia and Herzegovina in 1913

Year	Total production in BiH in quintals	Production in state-owned mines	The rest in quintals
1913	8,472	8,057,630	415.175

Source: Kemal Hrelja: "Industrija Bosne i Hercegovine do kraja Prvog svjetskog rata", (Industry of Bosnia and Herzegovina before the World War I", Belgrade 1961, p 47

The explanation of such involvement of the state in coal mining can be found in the Austro-Hungarian economic policy.

At the end of the nineteenth and at the beginning of the twentieth century coal was irreplaceable source of energy. It was used by railways, ships at the Adriatic Sea, and in manufacturing industry. Coal was a leverage in controlling railway and maritime transport and manufacturing industry. Benjamin Kallay made a concession to the private sector by transferring a burden of coal mining to the state. The government used coal mines with a view of improving finances of the country, and at the same time to help manufacturing industry by supplying it with a cheap coal. (Hrelja)

The following table shows a dynamic of growth of production of coal in a period 1885-1913:

Table 7 - Production of coal, its value, and the number of workers (1885-1913)

Year	Production of coal in quintals	Value in crowns	Number of employed workers
1885	230,091		76
1890	593,421		189
1895	1,954,419		727
1900	3,945,150		1,040
1905	5,402,336		1,525
1906	5,941,720	2,651,998	1,685
1907	6,211,788	3,016,371	2,129
1908	6,599,620	3,659,841	2,248
1909	6,691,140	3,846,334	2,526
1910	7,066,590	3,859,592	2,360
1911	7,697,628	4,618,768	2,756
1912	8,529,197	5,012,665	2,653
1913	8,472,805	5,091,971	2,669

SOURCE: LJUBOMIR KOSIER: "BiH-EKONOMSKI FRAGMENTI I KONTURE"(ECONOMIC FRAGMENTS AND CONTURES), p185-239; LAKATOS & DESPIC:" INDUSTRIJA BiH"(INDUSTRY OF BOSNIA AND HERZEGOVINA), p47, ZAGREB 1924; IZVJEŠTAJI ZAJEDNIČKOG MINISTARSTVA FINANSIJA O UPRAVI BiH GOD. 1906-1916 (REPORT OF THE COMMON MINISTRY OF FINANCE ON GOVERNING OF BOSNIA AND HERZEGOVINA YEAR 1906-1916); quoted from KEMAL HRELJA, op. cit. p 47

Using data in the table it is possible to calculate an average annual rate of growth of the coal mining industry in Bosnia and Herzegovina in a period 1885-1913 by using our formula (10).

$(\Delta Y + Y)/Y = (1 + g)^n$

$8{,}472{,}805/230{,}091 = (1 + g)^{28}$

$37 = (1 + g)^{28} /\log$

$\log 37 = 28 \log (1 + g)$

$1.56 = 28 \log (1 + g)/ : 28$

$1.56/28 = \log (1 + g)$

$0.056 = \log (1 + g)$

$(1 + g) = 10^{0.056}$

$g = 10^{1/18} - 1$

$g = 1.136 - 1$

$g = 0.136.$

The average growth rate of the coal mining industry in a period 1885-1913 was 13.6%.

Growth of the coal mining industry slightly outpaced the growth of manufacturing industry. Two factors contributed to this, a lack of competition, and low production costs, and therefore low prices of coal.

The table reveals disproportion between the rise in production and the rise in number of workers. The rise of workers outpaced the rise in production. As a result, production per worker decreased from 3.02 quintals per day in 1885 to 2.14 quintals per day. This is due to a reduction in working day from 13 to 9 hours. Labor productivity measured by output per worker hour remained roughly the same. Better mechanization and improved workers' skills were offset by exhaustion of rich layers of coal and exploitation of less rich coal deposits.

The largest proportion of coal was consumed in the country. Smaller quantities were exported to the Croatia proper,

Slavonia, and Hungary for steam mills, and in Serbia. Coal exploited in Kakanj, was of the best quality. It was exported via ports in Metkovic and Gruz, where it successfully competed with foreign companies and was used to supply ships with fuel. (Hrelja)

b) Iron mining

Bosnia and Herzegovina have a long tradition of iron mining, which goes back to the thirteen and fourteen centuries. A general inertia of the Ottoman economy was negatively reflected to the iron mining. The whole industry was reduced to several mines in Kresevo, Fojnica, Vares, and Stari Majdan, where primitive ovens were used to cast iron.

The law in 1869, whose aim was to modernize iron mining did not produce visible results because of inherent weaknesses of Turkish legislation and customs. The modern law was in collision with the Ottoman property legislation. The law was passed when there were not material conditions for its implementation. (Hrelja)

The Austro-Hungarian authorities started exploitation of iron ore in Vares in 1886, and in mine Ljubija in 1916, during the war. The real impetus to exploitation of iron ore in Vares was given in 1895 when two Vienesse banks, "*Unionbank*" and "*Wienerbankverein*" established a separate shareholding company which bought the mine from the government. The shareholding company both all equipment and foundries and smelters. Shareholding capital of this company amounted to 3,200,000 crowns, divided into 8,000 shares, each of them with a nominal value of 400 crowns. The company paid the government 4,250 shares. This means that the government owned 56% of the mine in Vares.

The thickness of the layers of iron ore in Vares mine was in the range of 20-200 meters with a width of 150 meters and length of 6 kilometers. Iron ore in Vares mine was of extremely high quality, with a content of iron ranging from 32-49%.

The following table shows dynamics of growth of production of iron ore in Vares mine:

Table 8 - Production of iron ore in Vares mine

Year	Iron ore in quintals	Value in crowns	Workforce
1880	23,050		
1895	127,302		
1900	1,334,543		
1905	1,225,396		
1906	1,365,131		
1907	1,506,841		
1908	1,149,868		
1909	1,200,692		
1910	1,397,208		
1911	1,397,730		
1912	1,594,200		
1913	2,191,314		

SOURCE: KEMAL HRELJA, op. cit. p 52

Using data in the table it is possible to calculate an average annual growth rate in production of iron ore.

$(\Delta Y + Y)/Y = (1 + g)^n$

$2,191,314/23,050 = (1 + g)^{33}$

$95 = (1 + g)^{33} /\log$

$1.98 = 33 \log (1 + g)/:33$

$\log (1 + g) = 1.98/33$

$\log (1 + g) = 0.06$

$(1 + g) = 10^{0.06}$

$(1 + g) = 10^{1/16.6}$

$g = 10^{1/16.6} - 1$

$g = 1.1487904 - 1$

$g = 0.149$

The average growth rate of iron ore production was almost 15% in a period 1880 – 1913. Growth was uneven. In the first decade of the twentieth century, it was almost stagnant. But vigorous growth in the last two decades of the nineteenth century and several years before the war produced more than impressive average growth rate which outpaced growth rates in coal mining and manufacturing industry.

The number of employees was constant for most of the years, but it almost doubled in the years before the war. Three fifths of iron ore was processed by smelter in Vares, and the remaining two fifths were exported to various smelters in the monarchy, the largest quantity to smelter in Servoli near Trieste. (Hrelja)

c) Non-ferrous metals

Exploitation of non-ferrous metals started in 1897 when the new mining cooperative "Bosnia" was established. It had a start-up capital amounting 1,720,000 crowns. The management was in the hands of the government, which owned 69% of its shares.

The cooperative consisted of the following mines: manganese mine in Semizovac-Cevljanovici, chromium mine in Dubostica, copper ore in Maskara, copper smelter in Sinjakovo, and old mines in Srebrenica, Olovo, and Cermenica. (Hrelja)

The following table shows the number of employees and the value of production of non-ferous metals.

Table 9 - Production, number of workers, and the value of production of manganese, chromium, copper, and mercury

Year	Production of cooper in quintals	Production of mercury in quintals	Production of manganese in quintals	Production of chromium in quintals	Value of production in crowns	Number of employees
1895						
1897			22,748			
1904			28,372			
1905	13,500	96	48,450	1,850		144
1906	7,650	51	41,290	3,200	284,936	336
1907	2,299	12	76,510	3,096	259,020	287
1908	110	50	70,000	4,996	302,185	293
1909	2,678	29	69,000	3,315	210,375	225
1910			56,920	3,200	135,040	178
1911			40,000	2,800	165,760	192
1912			52,000	2,000	115,300	133
1913			47,000	3,050	152,000	136

SOURCE: Izvještaj Zajedničkog ministarstva finansija o upravi u Bosni i Hercegovini u razdoblju 1906 – 1916 (Report of the Common Ministry of Finance on the governing of Bosnia and Herzegovina in a period 1906 – 1916), in I. Lakatos & A. Despic, quoted by Kemal Hrelja, op. cit. p 54

Only production of manganese and chromium recorded a rise. Production of copper ore fluctuated and stopped altogether in 1910. It contained a certain percentage of precious metals. Copper ore was exported via port Gruz to smelters in England. Manganese ore was exported to smelters in Trieste and glass smelters in Austria and Hungary. (Hrelja)

Hungarian mining-smelter shareholding company opened a mine of iron sulphid in Bakovici near Fojnica in 1984. Ore in mine in Bakovici contained 30 – 50% of sulfur. During the process of oxidation, it was turned into limonite, whose rinsing separated grains of gold (15 – 20 grams of gold in one ton on average).

Production of iron sulfide fluctuated year by year, recording an overall decrease from 190,450 quintals in 1905 to 77,014 quintals in 1913. (Hrelja)

The Bosnian magnesite shareholding company opened a magnesite mine in Zepce in 1908. Due to lack of capital production had been suspended on several occasions and even when there was a high demand for magnesite in the world market a total output was only 5,000 – 6,000 quintals. (Hrelja)

The overall poor performance of the non-ferrous metal sector could be explained by three factors: 1. Lack of capital, 2. Unfavorable location of mines, which increased transport costs, and 3. Sharp fluctuations of demand and prices in the world market.

d) Salt

The government purchased from families around Tuzla their inherited property rights on the production of salt and monopolized it. In Tuzla surroundings 16 wells were opened for exploitation of salted water. Each and every of them had a daily capacity of 2-2,500 hectoliters of salted water. In practice, though, only one fifth of its capacity was used. Salted water was extracted using electric pumps through wells deep 350-400 meters, and then taken to reservoirs. From the reservoirs salted water moved by gravity to saltworks where evaporation removed water and obtained salt. In 1884 the government built the first saltworks in Simin Han with six pens for boiling salt, with the area of 796 m^2 and two boilers for drying salt with the area of 1,760 m^2. The capacity of this saltworks was small, only 70,000 quintals of salt per annum. Eight years later another saltworks was built in Kreka, with far bigger capacity of 300,000 quintals per annum. This saltwork was also equipped better with more advanced technology. (Hrelja)

Both the saltworks processed only one third of salted water. The remaining salt water was taken by pipelines 14,5 kilometers long to ammoniac sodium factory in Lukavac.

The annual demand for salt in Bosnia and Herzegovina amounting 230-240,000 quintals was met by the production in Tuzla saltworks. (Hrelja)

The following table shows production of salt and the number of employees in saltworks:

Table 10 – Production of salt in quintals and the number of employees in saltworks in Bosnia and Herzegovina in a period 1905 – 1913

Year	Production of salt in quintals	Number of employees in wells and saltworks
1905	202,886	238
1906	226,710	248
1907	211,479	252
1908	193,819	243
1909	221,283	247
1910	235,792	243
1911	224,472	240
1912	231,244	203
1913	241,757	203

SOURCE: Izvještaj o upravi Bosnom i Hercegovinom (Report on governing Bosnia and Herzegovina), p 462, quoted by Kemal Hrelja, op.cit. p 56

The table reveals two things; 1. Fluctuations in production of salt with an overall rising trend, 2. A fall in number of employees, which is the result of implementation of more modern equipment and possibly increased proficiency of workers, leading to a higher labor productivity.

Using data in the table it is possible to calculate an average annual growth rate in production of salt in a period 1905 – 1913.

$(\Delta Y + Y)/Y = (1 + g)^n$

$(241,757)/(202,886) = (1 + g)^8$

$1.20 = (1 + g)^8 / \log$

$0.08 = 8 \log (1 + g) /:8$

$\log (1 + g) = 0.01$

$(1 + g) = 10^{0.01}$

$g = 10^{0.01} - 1$

$g = 1.023 - 1$

$g = 0.023$

Average growth rate in production of salt in a period 1905 - 1913 was 2.3%. A steady growth in production of salt fits into a pattern of a changing diet in low-income countries which experienced a rapid industrialization and urbanization.

MANUFACTURING INDUSTRY

Theoretical models and industry location

a) Theoretical models

Governors of Bosnia and Herzegovina, with the exception of Leon Bilinski, who was a professional economist, and who gain a lot of experience as the governor of the Austrian bank and the Austrian minister of finance, where not trained economists. Therefore, their decisions as regards economic policy and industrialization of Bosnia and Herzegovina were pragmatic and haphazard. Nevertheless, from this point of view, a combination of several theoretical models, most of which did were unknown at the time, could be revealed:

1. Mercantilism. Some of the characteristics of Mercantilism include a strong government involvement in the economy, low tariffs on imports of raw materials and semi-finished goods, high tariffs on imports of finished goods, and the use of colonies as sources of raw materials and markets for finished products. All these elements were very much present in the strategy of industrialization in Bosnia and Herzegovina. The country was incorporated in the Monarchy's customs union in 1880. This enabled Austrian manufacturing industry a cheap access to vital raw materials, and protection of foreign competition in using the Bosnian market for its finished products.

2. Soviet/Nazi model of a planned economy. The Soviet Union and the other communist countries applied the strategy of economic development in which industry was a leading sector, with a neglect of agriculture. Within industry the primacy was given to a heavy industry. This was in accordance with Marx's division of the economy on the sector A, which produces capital goods, and the sector B, which produces consumer goods, the idea which he took from the German economist Wolfgang Hoffman. The sector A is more technologically advanced part of the economy and therefore needs to have the primacy in industrialization (Mahmutefendic). This model was applied in Bosnia and Herzegovina, where manufacturing industry grew by the average annual growth rate of 12.4%, heavy industry by more than 15%, and agriculture by less than 1%. However, unlike the Soviet Union, where almost all means of production where nationalized, in

Bosnia and Herzegovina transportation, mining and manufacturing industry were state-owned, while most of enterprises were privately owned, with a lot of government indirect involvement. In addition, Istvan Burian, Kallay's successor, planned public works worth 182 million crowns (Sugar). All these resembles Nazi economic policy in the 1930's.

3. H-O-S theory of foreign trade – Herschel-Ohlin-Samuelson theory of foreign trade. Relatively modern version of the theory of comparative advantage, which was formulated in the 1930's. Named after its main contributors, two Swedish economists and Paul Samuelson, a Nobel Prize winner for Economics. This theory explains specialization in international trade according to a country's endowment with factors of production. The H-O-S theory suggests that countries with rich land resources should specialize in agriculture, mining and forestry, those with an abundance of labor should specialize in light industry, and countries rich with capital should specialize in production and export of capital equipment, chemicals and electronic products. (Mahmutefendic)

Bosnia and Herzegovina have plenty of wood, mineral ores, and coal. Extensive use of land as a factor of production fits into the H-O-S theory.

Lewis model – A theory of economic development set out in the 1950s by Sir Arthur Lewis, a Nobel Prize winner for Economics, originally from Saint Lucia. He noticed that developing countries were characterized by a dual economy, with a parallel existence of a capitalist and a subsistence sector. The subsistence sector is stagnating with the marginal product of labor being zero because of underemployment. The capitalist sector, which can be either privately or publicly owned and which consists of manufacturing industry, mining and plantations can draw on an unlimited supply of labor from the subsistence sector willing to work at the going wage rate. The capitalist sector will grow, increasing productivity and reinvesting profits and relying on abundant pool of labor in the subsistence sector. When all surplus of labor in the subsistence sector is eventually exhausted wages will start rising in the capitalist sector.

Although large chunks of the Bosnian economy were sucked into the market and moneyed economy, its lion's share was still in a subsistence economy. This part of the economy suffered from underemployment, primitive technical methods and a low productivity. At the same time advanced exporting sector was developed in which production rose at high rates in-spite of the fact that working hours were reduced from 13 to 9.

Keynesian deficit financing during Kallay's administration. Benjamin Kallay was a very ambitious man. He set three targets for Bosnia and Herzegovina; 1. To increase the standard of living, 2. To improve education of the population, and 3. To assure the self-governance for the country. During his administration industrial production grew at a staggering average annual rate of 15%. Although the government budget showed a small surplus for the whole period of his administration, there are serious doubts as regards the accuracy of the figures. Many expenditures were not recorded to portray the budget much better than it was. His successor Istvan Burian stated that the expenditures had reached such proportions that they threatened the whole economic development. Burian improved public finance, but at the expense of a slower growth. During his administration industrial production rose at an average annual growth rate of 8.4%, and in the last three years before the war at only 3.3%. (Palairet). An inverse correlation between the growth dynamics and state of the budget are the best proof of deficit financing strategy during Kallay's administration.

b) Industrial location

Industrial location is determined by a set of economic, political, cultural, social, and historical factors. The most important economic factors in determining where to locate a particular company are:

- Access to transport network
- Locally based input suppliers
- A pool of labor
- Sources of raw materials
- Closeness to markets
(Wall)

The location of heavy industry was often based on the notion of *bulk increasing* or *bulk decreasing* goods. This meant that if the industrial process gained weight, it would be located as near to the market as possible, whereas if it lost weight in the process it would be located as near to the source of raw materials as possible. Soft drinks production gains weight and is located near the market, whereas heavy industry significantly reduces weight and is placed near the source of its main raw materials – coal, iron and limestone. (Lines, Marcouse & Martin).

Mining and wood industry generate bulk decreasing goods. Therefore, their production capacities were located near sources of raw materials and transportation network. Mines were opened near the sources of mineral ores. At the same time factories which processed these ores were built close to the mines. This was the case with the Vares iron ore mine and the Vares ironworks, and the factory of ammoniac sodium in Lukavac. However, poor or non-existent transportation network prevented exploitation of rich layers of bauxite ore in Herzegovina and coal in North-East of Bosnia. (Hrelja)

The main criteria in location of chemical industry should be a closeness to the market and a closeness to the pool of skilled labor. In Bosnia, this principle was neglected and the closeness to the source of raw materials prevailed. A factory of caustic sodium was built in Lukavac, near rich sources of raw materials in-spite of the lack of transportation network and skilled labor. The same applies to wood distillery in Teslic, in Northern Bosnia, which had beech trees in abundance. Teslic had an additional advantage that it was close to a thermal power plant, which used a brown coal from a nearby coal mine. Unskilled labor was supplied from surrounding villages, whereas skilled labor was imported from Austria and Hungary. (Hrelja)

Hydro power plant in Jajce was a decisive factor in location of carbide factory in this town. Transport links, pool of labor, and source of raw material (salt was supplied from a saltworks in Tuzla) were neglected.

A chemical factory "Vila" was built in Sarajevo, due to a closeness to the market. But a chemical factory "Danica", an oil refinery in Bosanski Brod, was built with a neglect of all factors which could positively influence its location. This enterprise was erected hundreds of kilometers from its source of raw materials, Galician and Rumanian oil rigs, far from the pool of skilled workforce, in the largest agricultural region in Bosnia, which reduced the inflow of unskilled labor, and far from the world market, with a weak local market. Nevertheless, this enterprise was growing and was profitable due to its membership in a monopolistic cartel. (Hrelja)

Food processing industry was located near markets. Brewery in Sarajevo, a big colonial enterprise, was located in the capital of the province only because of its closeness to the market, while a sugar factory was built in Usora, close to a prospective source of a sugar beet, whose cultivation was encouraged, with poor results.

A steam mill produced losses because it was located far from the source of raw materials (wheat), while a factory of tinned vegetables, located in Alipasin Most near Sarajevo, failed because it depended on imports of vegetables from Slavonia and for the fact that market was narrow since the population of Sarajevo was not used to consume tinned vegetables.

Some enterprises were built for political reasons irrespective of economic factors of location. This applies to a tobacco factory, and a textile factory which were built in Sarajevo, with a view of employing poor and unskilled local labor. Ironworks in Vares was built partly because of the pressure exerted by Josip Stadler, the archbishop of Sarajevo, because a cathedral was erected in the town. (Hrelja)

In spite of failures in industry location, many companies worked profitably due to a set of favorable circumstances such as low railway tariffs, almost free raw materials, cheap local unskilled workforce, and a membership in monopolistic cartels.

In conclusion, one could say that industrialization of Bosnia and Herzegovina was conducted by a foreign capital in a near colonial circumstances, in which it was not clear to whom the province belongs, with a view of investing a surplus of capital and earning as high profit as possible. This shaped an anarchistic location of a manufacturing industry in which some areas remained without any industry and unconnected to the provinces transport network. (Hrelja)

Heavy industries

a) Metallurgy

Administrators of Bosnia and Herzegovina were aware of the great natural wealth in iron ore and a huge potential for developing metallurgy in Bosnia and Herzegovina. Hungarians, and to a lesser degree Austrians, wanted to use Bosnian iron ore for its smelters and to prevent a development of smelters on the territory of Bosnia and Herzegovina. This led to long-term disputes as regards the use of iron ore dug in Bosnia and Herzegovina, a spread of smelters in the country, and unexplainable failure in opening a iron mine in Prijedor, when the mine in Vares was showing signs of exhaustion. (Palairet)

The *Landsregirung* gave all important sources of iron ore to the company *Gewerkschaft Bosnia,* in which it had 20% of shares. This company was privately owned only on paper, in formal legal terms. The Bosnian company transferred its concessions for exploitation of iron ore to "*Vareser Eisenindustrie AG*", in which the government had 53% of shares, whereas the remaining shares were in possession of one Viennese bank. This company had a virtual monopoly in exploitation of iron ore in Vares eliminating competition, and establishing a profitable business. When ironworks in Zenica was established in 1892 the government had also 25% of shares while administration and highly ranked civil servants were significant co-owners. (Palairet)

Metallurgy in Bosnia and Herzegovina was, therefore, represented by two companies, in Vares and in Zenica. Vares was the first of the two enterprises to be established. The Ministry, which rejected an initial plan submitted by *Gewerkschaft Bosnia*" in 1884, later started operations under its own management with a capital of 850,000 florins. The plant opened in 1891. It was not clear how production could begin in 1891 when the mine legally still belonged to the community of Vares. In 1893 this company accepted from the *Landesregierung* a rent of 2.5 kreuzer for each quintal of ore mined for 40 years and granted the government exclusive mining rights. In 1893 the community received the small amount of 450 florins for the 18,000 quintals of ore mined. (Sugar)

In 1895 the government wanted to expand the plant and the production at Vares. It needed additional capital. As a result, *Vareser Eisenindustrie A.G."* was established with a capital of 1,600,000 florins. The government owned 4,250 shares, while the *Wiener Bankverein* owned the remaining 3,750 shares. The shareholders were guaranteed by the corporation an annual return of at least 4.5% and the bank became the company's exclusive banker. The *Landesregierung* paid the company annual rent of 83,200 florins and continued to manage the enterprise. The net profit remaining after the payment of the guaranteed interest, or any other rate the company saw fit to pay to shareholder, over this rate, was split, one third going to the *Landesregierung* and two thirds to the corporation. The *Landesregierung* had three men on the company's board of directors, the bank had two. (Sugar)

The second enterprise in Zenica was established in 1892 under the name *Eisen und Stahlgewerkschaft* with a capital of 400,000 florins. The government had only 25% share in the company. The biggest shareholder was a rich merchant from Prague, who contributed 70,000 florins in cash and 50,000 florins worth of machinery and equipment. The iron and steel mill, M.Schmid and Sons, in Wilhelmsburg, lower Austria, had a share equal to that of the government, and one of the Schmid sons, Adolf, became the manager of the Zenica enterprise. The remaining shares belonged to another Austrian steel mill, owned by Mr. Johann Pengg in Thorl, Styria. The Zenica establishment used the products of Vares to manufacture sheet metal, rails, bars and other finished iron and steel products. (Sugar)

Ironworks in Vares maintained continuity with a previous successful production. In years 1890-91, and 1896-1898 two blast furnaces, one foundry, and two furnace domes were built. Blast furnaces melt iron ore. Ironworks in Zenica was connected to the Vares company and used most of its iron ore. The rest was sold to ironworks and steelworks in other parts of the Monarchy. Foundries produced various iron products such as water pipes, ovens, and other cast which were produced by order. (Hrelja)

The Zenica enterprise used iron ore from Vares and coal extracted in a nearby coal mine, the only one in Central Bosnia.

Raw steel in the Zenica ironworks was produced in three Siemens-Martin blast furnaces built in 1898,1901, and 1913, with the annual capacity of 500,000 quintals of steel. Steel rolling was conducted on four rails, which used steam and electric power of 2,800 horse powers. Electric energy was obtained from its thermos power plant, whose two generators produced 2,000 horse powers. (Hrelja)

The following table shows the production and the value in the two companies and the number of employees:

Table 11 – Production and its value and the number of employees in Zenica and Vares ironworks

YEAR	PRODUCTION OF PIG IRON IN VARES IN QUINTALS	PRODUCTION OF SADIRON IN VARES IN QUINTALS	PRODUCTION OF ROLLED GOODS IN ZENICA	THE VALUE OF ROLLED GOODS IN CROWNS	THE NUMBER OF EMPLOYEES
1895	26,688	10,387	37,214		
1905	430,739	39,514	228,232	4,893,217	1,162
1906	456,253	48,613	254,991	5,561,887	1,173
1907	489,233	50,721	242,332	5,867,992	1,267
1908	516,280	46,126	271,849	6,218,057	1,332
1909	490,199	46,768	223,072	4,712,951	1,244
1910	488,105	50,905	273,632	5,426,044	1,153
1911	452,210	58,310	305,757	6,259,838	1,224
1912	532,700	67,010	327,906	7,274,830	1,293
1913	535,070	64,170	265,800	6,191,044	1,243

SOURCE: Izvještaj o upravi Bosnom I Hercegovinom godine 1906-1916 (Report on governing Bosnia and Herzegovina), Lakatos & Despic, op.cit, quoted from Kemal Hrelja, op.cit, p 63

Using the data in the table it is possible to calculate the average annual growth rate for the three products.

1. Pig iron

$(\Delta Y + Y)/Y = (1 + g)^n$.

$(535,070)/(26,688) = (1 + g)^{18}$

$20 = (1 + g)^{18} / \log$

$\log 20 = 18 \log (1 + g)$

$1.30 = 18 \log (1 + g)$

$\log (1 + g) = 0.072$

$(1 + g) = 10^{0.072}$

$(1 + g) = 1.18$

$g = 1.18 - 1 = 0.18$,

or rate of growth of 18% per annum.

2. Sadiron

$(\Delta Y + Y)/Y = (1 + g)^n$.

$(64,170)/10,387 = (1 + g)^{18} /\log$

$\log 6 = 18 \log (1 + g)$

$0.80 = 18 \log (1 + g)$

$0.022 = \log (1 + g)$

$(1 + g) = 10^{0.022}$

$g = 1.05 - 1$

$g = 0.05$,

or an average annual growth rate of 5%

3. Rolled goods

$(\Delta Y + Y)/Y = (1 + g)^n$.

$(265,800)/(37,214) = (1 + g)^{18}$

$7 = (1 + g)^{18} /\log$

$\log 7 = 18 \log (1 + g)$

$0.85 = 18 \log (1 + g)$

$(1 + g) = 10^{0.018}$

$(1 + g) = 1.042$

$g = 0.042$,

or the average annual growth rate was 4.2%.

In addition to the two ironworks, there was a small metal-processing firm, a factory of wires and nails, owned by Racher and Babic, in Sarajevo. The factory was a part of wholesale, merchant and service enterprise, with an annual capacity of 80 wagons of iron products. The enterprise employed around 60 workers. It had 65 machines used for drawing wires and production of nails. It was run by a steam energy of 110 horse powers. (Hrelja)

c) Chemicals

Bosnia and Herzegovina had also rich resources of limestone, hydro-energy, and rock salt, which enabled the development of a chemical industry. The chemical industry developed several plants, which turned raw materials into various products such as ammoniac sodium, caustic sodium, and calcium carbide. Small quantities of chemical products such as soap were made for domestic market. (Palairet)

The chemical industry was entirely in the hands of private businessmen. The four chemical plants which were established enjoyed numerous privileges and concessions granted by the government. Three of the four used domestic raw materials; the fourth had to import them. (Sugar)

The first of these factories, the *Erste Bosnische Ammoniaksodafabrik A.G.,* was established in 1894 in the small town of Lukavac, in North-East of Bosnia, 13 kilometers from the salt springs of *Donja Tuzla.* The Austrian Minister of Finance wanted to prevent opening of the factory arguing that soda factories in the Monarchy already produced more soda than it was needed. According to the Minister of Finance the soda factory in Lukavac had its economic rationale only if it produced soda for exports outside of the Monarchy since domestic market was weak to absorb the entire production and exports to the other parts of the Monarchy would increase the already present plight of the existing factories since the market was oversupplied. (Sugar)

In spite of this, Max Landau, a professional chemist, and the manager of the Viennese branch of the *Societe Lyonaise des Mines et Usines de Borax*, went ahead with the establishment of an ammonium soda plant in Bosnia and Herzegovina, and that he and his associates would provide the needed capital. Landau got his charter and privileges from the Common Ministry of Finance. These privileges included a fifty-year monopoly on soda production with an option for thirty more years; construction materials to be supplied by the government; the *Baudepartment* to build the factory on credit; supplies of brine and coal at costs prices for fifty years, and the lowest tariff rates by the railways for all shipments from and to the factory. Landau and his associates, the chemical companies Hassberg and S. Geiringer in Vienna and Peter Herzog, Eduard Landauer, and Heinrich Brull, industrialists, in Budapest, then established their enterprise with a capital of 700,000 florins, and their plant began to produce soda in 1895. A pipeline brought the brine from the salt springs to the factory, and Kreka, even nearer to Lukavac than Donja Tuzla, supplied the needed coal. During its first year of operation the factory used more than half a million hectoliters of brine, but in-spite of this large- scale production ended up the year with a loss of nearly 60,000 florins. Landau complained to Kallay that the loss was the result of the Austro-Hungarian soda factories lowered the price of soda from 8.50 florins to only 4.80 florins for 100 kilograms in order to drive the new competitor out of the business. Landau's appeal for help from the government was turned down since the latter already was working on a very tight budget. The help arrived in different form. On Kallay's insistence the factory was accepted to the soda cartel. As a result, the corporation's balance sheets showed that its capital had increased by 400,000 florins and that the business year closed with a net profit of almost 170,000 florins. By 1899 the plant was producing 27,000 metric tons of different qualities of sodas, and a year later, expecting the dissolution of the cartel in 1901, it was reorganized and its capital was increased once again, this time by an additional 1,000,000 crowns. In 1901 Kallay proudly announced that the Lukavac factory was one of the largest and best-equipped plants in the entire Monarchy. By 1904 the net profit of the enterprise amounted to more than 1 million crowns.

The figures for 1906 are even more impressive. During this year Lukavac bought, through a holding company which was incorporated in Hungary, the *Erste Bosnische Mineralolprodukten* und *Chemikalienfabrik* "Danica" for 3 million crowns. In spite of this, the shareholders earned 6% regular and 19% extra dividends on a net profit of more than 1.6 million crowns. The factory became so strong that it could have dominate the Monarchy's market in-spite of the fact that it stayed out of a newly created soda cartel. It shipped soda to the Monarchy in the following amounts; 13,466,400 kilograms in 1908; 15,227,500 kilograms in 1909; and 14,224,600 kilograms in 1910. (Sugar)

The Danica, which Lukavac purchased in 1906, was an oil refinery, the only industry of the province that relied on imported raw materials for its operations. The owners of the refinery were again Max Landau and his associates, and Dr Josepf Kranz. The owners wanted to secure the entrance of the refinery into the Monarchy's oil cartel. The corporation which was established in 1894, obtained significant privileges: free land on which to build the refinery; railway sidings and shipping piers built by the government at its own expense; assurance of special coal prices; and a monopoly of the Bosnia-Herzegovinian market. Lower railway rates were also included in the agreement. By 1898-1899 the Danica produced 17,243 metric tons of various oil products, but as it could not sell them in the Monarchy because of the resistance of the Austrian and Hungarian cartels which prevented the corporation's entrance into the market, it generated losses for many years. This finally led to the merger of the Danica with the plant at the Lukavac, which was easy to achieve since both the establishments were owned by the same individuals. By 1909, when it was admitted to the Hungarian cartel the Danica ceased to produce losses. (Sugar)

The establishments in Bosanski Brod and Lukavac were in the hands of the Monarchy's subjects. The other two chemical plants of Bosnia and Herzegovina were the creations of German capital, although Dr Kranz had a prominent role in the both, acting as their spoke person in the Ministry. The *Bosnische Holzverwertungs A.G.* in Teslic and the *Bosnische Elektrizitats A.G.* in Jajce were very substantial enterprises: both got their capital from the *Leipziger Bank*, both used wood as their raw material; both plants were established in 1897.

The factory in Teslic was more important of the two. Dr Kranz began working in 1895, and secured for himself the right to exploit the forests around Teslic and in the valley of the Usora river. Kranz got considerable privileges from the Ministry. They included the following: paying as little as 30 kreuzers for a cubic meter for beech trees; obtaining for as little as 22 kreuzers for 100 kilograms of Kreka coal delivered at the plant; a special railway freight rate of 1.25 kreuzer per 100 kilograms per a kilometer for all shipments coming and going to the factory; and the promise that the ironworks of Vares would buy all the charcoal produced in Teslic for 13 florins per ton F.O.B. the production site.

The factory in Teslic consisted of distillery plants, a main workshop, a workshop for fixing wagons and locomotives, a lime pit of brown coal, and a sawmill. In the year 1902 the electric power with two driving machines was built, one run by a steam of 450 horse powers and one with absorbent gas of 320 horse powers, and two generators of 350 KW and 250 KW. (Hrelja)

The Teslic establishment manufactured wood alcohol, methanol, acetate of lime, turpentine, charcoal, tar oil, and acetone. The number of employees rose from 300 in 1899 to 3,500 in 1915, proving that this was a large enterprise. It was the largest acetone producer in the Monarchy with a yearly capacity of 1 million kilograms. (Sugar)

The fourth chemical enterprise, the *Bosnische Elektrizitats A.G.* in Jajce was established by Dr Kranz, the *Leipziger Bank,* and the Schuckert & Co. firm of Nurnberg. Kranz began his activities related to the establishment of the enterprise by obtaining the right to exploit the power of the great waterfall of Jajce and exchanged the concession for shares of the corporation, in the same way he used his wood concessions at Teslic with a similar aim. It is likely that the shares were equally divided between the three owners, with the Schukert taking over the *Leipziger Bank's* interest.

Kranz was permitted to establish an electrochemical plant at Jajce using the power of the waterfall to run the factory. The corporation started its operations with a capital of 3.5 million florins of which 1.6 million florins were to be used to build an electric power station. Kranz could not raise this amount, but was allowed to establish his corporation with a capital of 3 million florins, as the *Leipziger Bank* guaranteed to provide the remaining half a million florins. On the 1.6 million florins for the electric power station the government was to pay the corporation a 5% interest. The government was entitled to 20% of the corporation's net earnings, and to 2,000 horsepower of current free of charge. The government was also granted the right to buy the power plant, but in this case the factory was entitled to free electricity. The factory, which the founders were not allowed to sell for five years, was planned to produce various chemical products such as chloride of lime and potassium, sodium chloride, calcium carbide, and etching natron. It was given the usual monopoly rights which included free railway sidings, and freight rate advantages.

When in 1901, ten years after it had began producing, a deputy in the Delegations stated that the factory was a failure and operated with great losses, Kallay dodged the answer. Kallay must have had the information as regards the profit and loss account of the company since the government was entitled to 20% of its net profit. His evasive answer leads to a conclusion that the establishment must have been an unsuccessful venture. (Sugar)

Two other small establishment in chemical industry are worth mentioning. A soap and candles factory Vila was the first one of this type established in Bosnia and Herzegovina. Its built was prompted by a rapid urbanization and influx of soldiers, civil servants and other immigrants form the monarchy. This increased demand for the products of personal hygiene. In-spite of this consumption of soap was only 200 wagons a year, or around 1 kilogram of soap per person, compared to 4.5 kilograms for the whole monarchy. The reason for this lies in the fact that rural population traditionally used ashes for washing clothes whereas urban population was used to produce their own soap. The soap industry in Bosnia and Herzegovina remained underdeveloped because of a weak internal market and a strong competition from Austrian, Hungarian, and Croatian producers.

The Vila enterprise managed to resist the competition of producers in other parts of the monarchy and to be profitable due to low production costs. The enterprise was part of interest sphere of the Agrarian and Commercial bank of Bosnia and Herzegovina. (Hrelja)

The other chemical industry enterprise was Dr Vasic & Komp. From Visegrad. This establishment was built with a view of making turpentine and rosin from black pine, which Bosnia and Herzegovina possessed in abundance.

First extraction of rosin in Europe was established in Busovaca near Travni8k in 1912. Its founders were N. Majezha and Dr

Vasic. Using the experience in Bosnia two factories of rosin were built in Hungary, one in Poland and one in Lithuania. Bosnian output was sold in Austria. The factory had only one extractor, which was not sufficient. This is why Dr Vasic and Schmalzhofer established the same type of factory in Visegrad in 1914.

Chemical industry in Bosnia and Herzegovina had the largest concentration of capital and workforce. These establishments were in the hands of Austro-German entrepreneurs and were most of the time included in monopolistic cartels. This is why the chemical industry differ more from feudal surroundings compared to the other industries. (Hrelja)

Forestry

Wood was the most abundant raw material available in Bosnia and Herzegovina. Nearly half of the territory of the country was covered with forest. Three quarters of the land was owned by the state, which took over all forests owned by the Ottoman state and all holdings to which individual owners could not establish a clear title.

The government considered the forests not only a useful industry, but also the main source of its revenue. Modest revenues of the government prompted it to leave exploitation of the forests to private enterprises. By the pass of time this industry became the most important single sector of the country's industrial complex in terms of capital invested and the number of workers employed.

Forest exploitation occurred under the Ottoman rule but was limited almost entirely to the production of oak staves for barrels. The production of oak staves for barrels survived some time but faded away by the year 1904. It was replaced by other more complex and more modern products. Most of the large woodworking companies were established during the first half of the occupation period when the government was very hard up for revenue. The contracts which the government concluded with various private enterprises were long-term with the price fixed for the entire period of the contract and usually very low. This caused continuous and fierce attacks on the government by deputies in the Delegation. The government was criticized for bad management, favoritism, ruthless forest exploitation for small gains, insufficient supervision of forestry enterprises, and negligence in reforestation. (Sugar)

The private companies in the forestry operated on a high profit margin. For example, in 1904 the wood exports from Bosnia and Herzegovina amounted to more than half a million cubic meters. The price which the companies paid to the government was 1.05 crowns for a cubic meter, while a sale price amounted to almost 30 crowns per cubic meter. If we apply the formula for a mark-up and profit margin we arrive at:

1. Mark-up = (selling price − costs)/ costs x 100
   Mark -up = (29.30 − 1.05)/1.05 x 100
   Mark-up = 2825/1.05
   Mark-up = 2690%

2. Profit margin = (selling price − costs)/selling price x 100
   Profit margin = (29.30 − 1.05)/29.30 x 100
   Profit margin = 28.25/29.30 x 100
   Profit margin = 96%

The sawmills were in the forests, and thus the sales price did not include freight charges. Wages were low. Using the sales prices in Trieste Susteric, the deputy in the Delegation proved in 1906 that the Bosnian wood merchants undersold the Austrians 5 to 1. The ease with which the country's forest enterprises undersold the Austrians indicates that the country produced lumber cheaply.

The price policy was severely criticized as the one damaging the Monarchy's wood industry pointing out that the income the government derived from selling wood as cheaply as it did was not justifying the agreement with the forestry companies.

Huge disparities between the selling and the buying price of wood enabled the enterprises to extend their export sales from year to year. The following table shows a rise in the export sales:

Table12- Rise in export sales and value of wood from Bosnia and Herzegovina 1898-1911

YEAR	QUANTITY EXPORTED IN QUINTALS	VALUE OF EXPORTS IN CROWNS
1898	719,240	
1899	1,927,266	
1900	2,694,073	
1901	2,918,172	
1902	2,939,189	
1903	3,760,309	18,888,727
1904	4,866,160	23,266,838
1905	4,918,712	26,165,866
1906	5,606,992	28,109,340
1907	5,338,529	52,083,814
1908	5,465,040	31,704,177
1909	5,820,705	31,022,384
1910	5,369,399	32,196,044
1911	5,359,898	34,347,329

SOURCE: PETER SUGAR: "INDUSTRIALIZATION OF BOSNIA AND HERZEGOVINA 1878-1918", UNIVERSITY OF WASHINGTON PRESS 1963, p 133

The data in the table could be used to calculate an average growth rate of export sales of wood in a period 1898-1911.

$(\Delta Y + Y)/Y = (1 + g)^n$.

$(5,359,898)/719,240 = (1 + g)^{13}$

$7.45 = (1 + g)^{13}/\log$

$\log 7.45 = 13 \log (1 + g)$

$0.87 = 13 (1 + g)$

$\log (1 + g) = 0.87/13$

$\log (1 + g) = 0.067$

$1 + g = 10^{0.067}$

1 + g = 1.166

g = 1.166 -1

g = 0.166

The export sales of wood rose at the staggering average annual rate of 16.6%.

The Austrian forestry businessmen complained that a vigorous growth in Bosnian exports sales of wood reduced their exports sales by 20 to 25%. Burian defended the position of the Bosnian forestry industry claiming that the wood business was not only important as a valuable source of government revenue, which amounted to 8 to 9 million crowns, but also a provider of income for 20,000 workers. Furthermore, Burian pointed out, the country's exports did not go to northern Italy, Austria's main market, but to southern Italy (45%), western Europe (25%), North Africa (12%), Austria-Hungary (7%), other destinations (2.6%), with only a fraction (6.7%) going to northern Italy. Therefore, he claimed, the Bosnian exports could not be considered a threat to Austria's export trade.

All the figures related to the exports sales of the forestry industry show that this industrial branch grew to considerable proportions during the Austro-Hungarian period. In 1915 there were 34 joint stock forestry and lumber companies. (Sugar)

A turning point in lumber and forestry industry occurred in the beginning of the 1890's. The exhaustion of oak trees marked the end of the production of staves. The entrepreneurs then turned their attention to other kinds of trees. The alternative use of woods surpassed the stave industry in importance, making the lumber and forestry industry into the most important production sector of the country.

Several native capitalists participated in the lumber business, but with little success. A lack of capital and business connections, particularly in the foreign markets, limited their role to supply of the domestic market.

Foreign capitalists established large and very important companies producing building materials, wood for carpenters and furniture manufacturers, and even some timber for ships. These giant enterprises were almost entirely export-orientated.

The biggest three companies in this industry were *Bosnisch-Hercegovinische Forstindustrie A.G,* Otto Steinbeis, a German enterprise; Eisler and Ortlieb, half German and half Austrian owned; and Fratelli Feltrinelli, an Italian corporation from Milan.

The biggest enterprise was established by a Bavarian entrepreneur and capitalist Otto Steinbeis in 1892. He signed a thirty-year contract covering the forests of the large area lying roughly in the triangle between Drvar, Jajce, and Doberlin in the surroundings of Banjaluka, Bihac and Travnik. This area amounted to 45,000 hectares and contained some 18,000,000 cubic meters of usable wood. He paid 1.00 florin for each cubic meter of wood. Steinbeis erected numerous sawmills, and other woodworking establishments. He built two railways, Drvar-Jajce, and Prijedor-Knin, totaling 375.3 kilometers, connecting its possessions with the Banjaluka-Doberlin line and this with railways in Italy, Austria, and Germany. In Sebenico, in Italy, he built his own port installations and even owned 4,000-ton ship. He had his own housing projects, schools, hospitals for his workers, his own private roads, and a cellulose factory worth 3 million crowns. This factory was located in the town of Drvar in northwestern Bosnia and had a yearly capacity of 12 million kilograms of cellulose, and began to operate in May 1907. The factory used the waste of the various other Steinbeis companies as raw material. Dr Josef Kranz got permission from Kallay to establish the factory. (Sugar)

Steinbeis' forests and mills employed 3,000 workers on the average. The establishment was successful and profitable, earning a net profit of 4% in the first ten years of its existence. In 1900 he transformed his company into a corporation with a nominal capital of 8 million crowns divided into 40,000 shares with a face value of 200 crowns, but issued only 30,000 shares of which he owned 60%, or 18,000. Dr Josef Kranz was the second largest shareholder owning 3,250 shares, and a certain Wilhelm Spitzer the third with 3,000 shares.

In 1912, when he was 73 years old, Steinbeis decided to sell his enterprise. His establishment was liquid, since the value of its assets amounted to almost 30 million crowns, whereas total liabilities were around 12 million crowns, of which 3 million crowns represented the capital of the cellulose factory, 2.6 million crowns were owed to the Union bank and *Wienerbankverein,* and 3.65 crowns were owed to the government. The only possible buyer was the government, which bought out two the other big shareholders, Dr Kranz and Spitzer. This was an attractive deal for the government, since the enterprise was successful making a gross profit of more than 2.5 million crowns in 1912, the last year it was privately owned.

By the end of the WWI the government owned and controlled all the enterprises in the industry since it confiscated the Italian company when Italy entered the war on the side of the Entente. (Sugar)

Production of matches belongs to this branch of industry in a broader context. The first matches factory was established in Dolac near Travnik. The factory enjoyed less privileges than the government normally granted industrial enterprises. Nevertheless, it established itself and managed to survive.

Another match factory was established in 1900 by a group of Sephardic Jew capitalists consisting of S.D.Alkalay, J.M. Israel, J.D. Salom, and I.G. Salom, who asked the government for permission to establish the *Erste Bosnisch-Hercegovinische Zundwarenfabrik.* The applicants collected 100,000 crowns and hired an Austrian expert F. Kolb, as manager. They asked the government to allow them to buy the empty factory building which was left behind in Dolac by a leather manufacturer who gave up his business for the cot of 10,000 to 12,000 crowns.

Their calculations had shown that they needed 42,700 crowns to purchase needed machinery. They planned to produce 14,600,000 boxes of matches, one fifth of the total consumption of matches in the country, for 93,440 crowns and sell it for 119,720 crowns. They envisaged to employ 40 to 50 workers. (Sugar)

The government accepted the proposal and sold the building for 10,000 crowns, conditioning that the factory should produce only safety matches. Alkalay became the manager and the establishment of factory went ahead in-spite of imposed limitation. Austrian producers of matches complained of the competition coming from the factory. They claimed that the Bosnia-Herzegovina matches industry not only excluded Austrian products from a domestic market but also begun to compete with the Austrian industry in Austria proper. This would have been acceptable if it had not been due to privileges the government granted the Bosnian producers. These privileges included a 50% reduction of railway freight rates on domestic and a 75% reduction on export shipments. Burian defended the government position pointing out that the Bosnia factory was too small to compete with Austrian producers, and that although Bosnia-Herzegovina was an integral part of the Monarchy's customs union, each government had the right to grant tariff privileges to the home industry.

The establishment was a success in-spite of the limitation imposed by requiring only the production of safety matches, and the fact that the building burn down in 1905. The owners managed to expand production and increase the capital of corporation to 600,000 crowns in 1910. This is due to the fact that the match factory was carefully planned, started on a modest scale, and was managed by an expert. When production of safety matches was imposed to all producers in the Monarchy, the Bosnian factory's future was assured. (Sugar)

Textile industry

Bosnia and Herzegovina had excellent natural conditions for the development of a textile industry. This is because it had developed cattle breeding, which enabled production of needed raw materials, particularly wool, whose yearly output amounted to 1,000,000 kilograms. (Sugar). In-spite of this the Bosnia textile industry was limited to several small factories. Production of textile goods on a large scale was prevented by two factors: 1. Economic policy of the Monarchy, and 2. Narrow local market. (Hrelja)

There were attempts by entrepreneurs from the other parts of the Monarchy to establish big textile factories in Bosnia and Herzegovina. Two examples illustrate the failure of their attempts as a result of wrong economic policy decisions. Benjamin Kallay invited Mr Carl Low, the famous Bohemian textile manufacturer, who supplied 35% of the woolens used by the Austro-Hungarian army and had several big mills in Russia. Low was interested. He suggested the government that Sarajevo was the only suitable place for a textile mill because it had best communications, was the main market place in the country, and was the wool trade center of Bosnia and Herzegovina. He also was of the opinion that the mill should produce coarse woolens which the local population preferred. According to him production had to be directed towards satisfying the local demand and that of the neighboring countries and provinces who used the same type of cloth which was popular in Bosnia and Herzegovina. Yet the production had to remain below the need of the local market, because ruining the household industries would bankrupt prospective customers. Low submitted elaborate and detailed plan asking for modest privileges, which should have been acceptable to the government. For some reason, Kallay did not like his proposal and the plan of building a big textile mill was ditched. (Sugar).

Two large companies, Julius Mayer of Vienna and Alois Schumpeter & Sohn in Triesch (Moravia), proposed to establish a complex of six factories in Bosnia and Herzegovina for the production of military clothing supplies. Three plants were supposed to produce woolens, linens, and leather, while the other three would have manufactured cloth, blankets, underwear, shoes, and harnesses from the products of the first three establishments. These two businesses not only offered both construction and working capital, but they were willing to deposit a guarantee of 20,000 florins. They asked only for privileges usually granted to industrial enterprises in Bosnia and Herzegovina, i.e., cheap freight rates, low coal prices, a fifteen-year tax exemption, and the promise, that should their prices and quality be in line with those offered by the competitors, the government would give them the contracts which would be involved. The Ministry answered with a delay, granting the privileges, but only under the conditions that Mayer and Schumpeter acquire a construction site in the country within three months. In addition, the Ministry required a deposit of 50,000 florins, un-refundable if the three conditions were not met. This put off Mayer and Schumpeter who consequently withdrew. (Sugar).

Weak internal market prompted government decision makers to support the branches of a textile industry which would use domestic raw materials, and which would produce goods for local population, and possible surpluses for exports. Benjamin Kallay, built a carpet and rug factory, and embroiderer in Sarajevo with this intention. The first establishment was built in 1888 and the second one in 1892. The carpet and rugs factory had a modest start employing 30 workers in 1892, but grew to a big enterprise with 400 employees in 1910. The factory expanded territorially and opened branches in several towns in the country such as Kresevo, Fojnica, Foca, Cajnice, Jelec, Kladanj, Glamoc, and Visoko. A growth of the establishment was boosted by an external demand for its products, particularly in Austria and Germany.

A weaving mill had 12 looms for Persian carpets, 146 looms for Bosnian carpets and one loom for embroidery. The workforce was provided by local poor population. In Sarajevo work was performed in the headquarters of the enterprise, while in the branches throughout the country a household work was conducted.

In embroiderer different types of domestic and decorated linen were produced, but also decorated embroiders for clothes and furniture. This establishment used a household work. These two establishments were an example of a capitalist manufacture in which the capitalist, in this case the state, exploited poor rural and urban population. (Hrelja)

There were five more textile enterprises in Bosnia and Herzegovina which operated on the same principle.

- Elias E. Kabiljo, the merchant from Sarajevo, established an enterprise in 1910, which employed a household work to make weaving and embroidery products. This business particularly thrived during the WWI when it became the main supplier of goods from Istanbul. The enterprise grew in size to employ 2000 weavers and embroiders.
- Salom and his associate built the first manual and mechanical weaving mill in Sarajevo in 1910. The enterprise used 46 weaving looms to produce oriental goods.
- Risto Lj. Besarovic, the merchant from Sarajevo, built a cord factory in Sarajevo in 1885. In 1895 the factory was transferred to Kosevo brook so that it can use a waterfall energy. A water turbine of 25 horse powers set in motion 100 knitting machines. This enterprise made golden, silver, silk, and woolen cord, but did not use a half of its capacity due to a strong competition coming from Serbian and Bulgarian manufacturers of cheap goods.

- Avram Levi Sadic opened a socks factory in Sarajevo. The factory was opened in 1896 and remained a small establishment.
- Muhamed Uzicanin, a Bosnian Landowner, and his associate Bascausevic, opened a cloth and wool factory in Sarajevo in 1888. In this factory coarse fabric, covers and weaved wool were produced as semi-manufactured products used in the carpet factory. (Hrelja)

The episode with Uzicanin is worth mentioning as a proof of mistakes made in developing a textile industry by the authorities. In 1889 Uzicanin, a Bosnian landowner who had never been in the textile business before, received both a license and a 7,000 florins loan for the purpose of establishing a cloth and blanket factory in Sarajevo. He applied for another 8,000 florin-loan in December of the same year. His buildings had been erected by then, but not a single machine had been installed. Uzicanin was soon in financial troubles. He got an additional loan from the government to which he offered his sister's real estate as collateral. With additional funds secured he went ahead with his establishment. He refused to listen to the advice of the government engineers, bought too much equipment, much of which were useless, and failed to hire qualified workforce for his establishment. He was in trouble again. He blamed the intrigues of the large cloth importers for his failure, but never addressed his own mistakes. He was not liquid, but was solvent, since he owed the government and factories in Austria 31,000 florins, but had a real estate worth 44,000 florins. Because of this he applied for another loan from the government in the amount of 12,000 florins. The government concluded that the factory produced good merchandise, that it was useful, and that it should be granted an additional help, under the condition that the mill be put under the commercial and technical management of appointed experts.

After a year long deliberation Vienna made the decision to transform the establishment, under the management of an Austrian expert, into a spinning mill manufacturing yarn for the planned governmental rug factory. This plant was to rely on traditional skill of the local rug weavers and knotters to produce rugs and carpets for the Western European and Russian markets. To achieve this, it was planned to use traditional art of making Persian rugs. For this reason, a Persian painter was hired whose task was to make designs for oriental rug decoration. The result was satisfactory from a commercial point of view. The imitation Oriental rugs sold found their market, sales increased, and by 1901 it employed 209 weavers. In 1911 the factory contracted a 70,000-crown loan at 4.5% interest to expand even further. (Sugar)

There was another abortive attempt to establish textile mills in Bosnia and Herzegovina. In 1911 the *K.u.K. Privilegirte Bohmische* Union Bank sent an expert to Banjaluka, and in 1914 the government had reported that its study had proven that a textile industry should be established in the country as soon as possible. This plan never materialized. (Sugar)

Using capital invested, capacities, and workforce employed, a textile industry in Bosnia and Herzegovina remained in a rudimentary form. It employed only 2800 workers (Hrelja). Kallay's strange decisions, particularly the refusal of two offers from the Bohemian capitalists, Burian's opposition to the industrialization of the country, and Bilinski's late arrival to power, offer explanation for this. (Sugar)

Food-processing industry

Bosnia and Herzegovina did not have a natural base for the development of the food-processing industry. This is owing to unresolved agricultural relations and a highly extensive nature of the country's agriculture. The only two big food-processing enterprises were a brewery and a sugar factory, which operated using imported raw materials. They could be profitable only on the basis of benefits they were granted by the government and favorable developments in the market.

The other enterprises of food-processing industry such as those which produce alcohol, canning vegetables, mills and the capacities for processing plums were of a small size and had mostly a seasonal character.

Plums were very important for Bosnia and Herzegovina. They had the same significance for Bosnia as grapes for Herzegovina and wheat for Banat and Srem. Plums were grown on 80% of 44,113 hectares of the territory covered with orchards. An average annual yield was 1,3 million quintals, out of which 40% was used to make dry plums, 40% to make a plum brandy, 10% for making a marmalade, and 10% was used in afresh state. (Hrelja)

Grapes were grown in Herzegovina on the area of 6,200 hectares, and the yearly yield varied between 50,000 and 85,000 quintals.

The first stage in processing dried plums is etivage, which consists of sterilizing plums using a heat. The country's center of processing food was a town of Brcko. There were four establishment for this activity in 1910, producing in total 89,000 quintals of etivaged plums and employing 270 workers. In addition, there were four smaller establishments with a daily capacity of 50 quintals. This operation had a seasonal character and the output fluctuated year by year depending on the plum yield. Dried plums were exported mainly to Austria and Germany.

The following table shows sharp fluctuations in exports of dried plums from Bosnia and Herzegovina:

Table 13 – Exports of dried plums from Bosnia and Herzegovina (etivaged) 1905-1918

YEAR	IN QUINTALS	YEAR	IN QUINTALS	YEAR	IN QUINTALS
1905	51,000	1910	77,500	1915	29,000
1906	275,000	1911	114,000	1916	130,400
1907	50,800	1912	24,800	1917	76,500
1908	369,000	1913	236,500	1918	261,000
1909	25,100	1914	226,700		

SOURCE: Kemal Hrelja: "Industrija Bosne i Hercegovine do kraja Prvog svjetskog rata (Manufacturing Industry of Bosnia and Herzegovina until the WWI), Belgrade 1961, p87

In 1911 M. Fisla and Son opened "The first Bosnian factory and refinery of spirit in Kreka near Tuzla. The factory had a yearly capacity of 3 million liters and employed 120 workers.

There were around 9,000 small individual producers of alcohol. They used plums, pitted fruit and wine alloy as raw materials.

A factory "Pehar" for canning vegetables was built in Cengic Vila near Sarajevo in 1910. The enterprise was organized as a limited company with a starting shareholding capital of 600,000 crowns. The establishment did not expand because of a strong competition from Austro-Hungarian producers and due to the fact that the market was narrow since local population was not accustomed to consume canned vegetables. In addition, raw materials were expensive since they were brought mainly from Slavonia. The enterprise employed around 100 workers. (Hrelja)

"Leopold Stockhammer" was the first vinegar factory in the country. The enterprise was built in 1902, produced around 5,000 liters a year, and employed 20 workers.

Steam mill was built in 1908 in Sarajevo. Shareholding capital of 750,000 crowns was invested to erect the factory with a capacity of 10,000 tons. However, only half of the capacity was utilized, because of damaging tax policy and a narrow market.

Two smaller factories were built, one in Banjaluka, owned by Maria Stern, with a capacity of 4,500 tons, and the one in Ukrina near Derventa, with a capacity of 3,500 tons.

The main problem of this branch of food-processing industry was a small market of rural population and the fact that urban population met its needs by imports from Slavonia and the southern Hungary. As a result of low domestic production, the imports of wheat and flour amounted to 18% of the total imports of the country. (Hrelja)

The oldest brewery in the country belonged to the Trappist monks in Travnik and was built before the occupation. In 1887, two Bohemians, the prune merchant, Kohn, and his brother-in-law, the brewer Taussig, had established a brewery in Tuzla with a production of 10,850 hectoliters yearly. There were three other breweries in Sarajevo with yearly production capacities of 7,482 hectoliters in Lovy's brewery, 4,060 hectoliters in Aschenbrenner's brewery, and 1,872 hectoliters in Kovacevic's brewery. The government forced the three brewers to merge. The new enlarged corporation had to make such a big profit to maintain itself and to support the bankrupt distillery in Tuzla, which was established in 1888, and which was bought by the government after generating losses for five consecutive years. In order to achieve this goal, the government introduced freight rates permitting the new corporation called Aktienbrauerei to compete with other breweries in the country while these other breweries could not compete with the Aktienbrauerei in Sarajevo. The corporation became the government's partner and bought the failing distillery in Tuzla. The plan proved to be sound. Having advantage in the market the new establishment managed to increase production to 30,600 hectoliters a year and to make a profit of 126,000 florins in 1894-95, while the distillery lost 82,000 florins. (Sugar)

Beer produced in Bosnia and Herzegovina was consumed partly by a local population, but more by immigrants such as soldiers and civil servants, while surpluses were exported to neighboring countries.

Aktienbrauerei-Spiritus merged with a sugar mill in Usora to create the A.G. fur *Verarbeitung und Verwertung Landwirtschaftlicher Produkte.* Prior to the establishment of the sugar mill Bosnia and Herzegovina imported 4,5 million kilograms of sugar per annum. The sugar mill was built with the aim of replacing the imports. The plan was to handle 50 million of kilograms of sugar beet. However, the factory's production never exceeded 1 million kilograms of sugar per year. Kallay was overoptimistic when he stated that in Bosnia 150 to 400 hundred-weights of beets could be produced per hectare, that the beets were excellent, and that the peasants who got 80 kreuzers per hundred-weight were pleased to plant this crop which had never been cultivated before. Unfortunately, the facts differed significantly from the figures given by Kallay. The beets were of poor quality, and the yield per hectare was only between 122 and 173 hundred-weights. The peasants received only 4 kreuzers per hundred-weight, 20 times less than Kallay envisaged. This price was lower than the price of any other crop. The peasants received 5 kreuzers for potatoes, 8 kreuzers for corn, and 6 to 10 kreuzers for cereals. In such a situation the government and the police had to use force to put the pressure on the peasants to continue with the production. As a result of these developments, although the government invested 400,000 florins in the sugar mill through the holding company the mill continued to generate losses. Only after 1910, when the mill became the member of the Hungarian sugar cartel, it started making a modest profit.

The sugar mill was too big for the small needs in Bosnia and Herzegovina. The mill was organized on the wrong assumption, which was maintained even after experience proved contrary, that the soil of the Posavina is suitable for sugar beets and that the peasants would be pleased to have an additional crop and that they would be therefore eager to cultivate it. Kallay misjudged the situation in his overzealous ambition to industrialize rapidly the country at any cost, regardless of particular circumstances. (Sugar)

Tobacco industry

The government monopolized the production and manufacturing of tobacco in 1880. The production of tobacco constantly grew to reach a yield of 40,000 quintals before the WWI. Planting and cultivation of tobacco employed around 20,000 workers, whose annual revenue ranged between 4 and 6 million crowns. The government organized manufacturing of tobacco in four factories and seven redemption and fermentation stations.

The following table shows the production and manufacturing of tobacco:

Table14 - Tobacco factories

Town	Year of factory building	Tobacco for smoking in quintals	Number of cigarettes	Number of employees
Sarajevo	1880	14,000	46,000,000	865
Mostar	1880	5,500	15,000,000	320
Banja Luka	1888	5,800	20,000,000	287
Travnik	1893	6,400	10,000,000	288

SOURCE: Kemal Hrelja:"Industrija Bosne i Hercegovine do kraja Prvog svjetskog rata (Manufacturing industry of Bosnia and Herzegovina until the World War I), Belgrade 1961, p 87

In redemption and fermentation stations 870 workers were employed. The total number of employees in the tobacco industry was 2,630.

The tobacco industry was a very important industrial branch in terms of generating a revenue. In 1909 a revenue and a profit from the tobacco industry amounted to 15,466,000 crowns and 7,516,000 crowns respectively. In the following years the profit rose to 9,000,000 crowns.

The tobacco industry was also a very important source of foreign currencies. Unprocessed tobacco was mainly exported to Egypt, while the main destinations for exports of manufactured tobacco were Austria, Hungary, and Germany. (Hrelja)

Paper industry

There were excellent conditions for developing a paper industry in Bosnia and Herzegovina. The country had a plenty of needed raw materials such as wood, coal and water. In-spite if this this industrial branch was represented only by two smaller enterprises.

Eduard Musil, the Viennese industrialist, made a 25-year agreement with the government to build a paper factory in Zenica and to become a sole provider of paper to the state institutions with pre-arranged fixed prices. Musil built the factory and started the production of paper for packaging using imported cellulose. Later this industrialist started buying a ready-made paper in Austria and sell it at higher prices in Bosnia and Herzegovina. When the contract with the government expired in 1910, he transferred the equipment to Vienna and sold the building to the Zenica mine.

S.D. Alkalaj established a factory in Sarajevo in 1905 which produced cigarette paper. The factory used imported raw materials to manufacture 200,000 packets of monopolistic and

150,000 packets of luxury cigarette paper. The enterprise employed around 60 workers. (Hrelja)

Graphic industry

There were 16 printing houses in the country. Their production exceeded the needs of a domestic market, so they supplied the other parts of the Monarchy by the order.

In 1866, before the occupation, Ignjat Sofron opened a workshop for stamping books. The government took it over after the occupation, expanded and modernize it
Milena Mrazovic opened the Bosnian Post printing house in 1883. This was the biggest and the most modern printing enterprise in the country equipped with rotation for newspapers and magazines, and machines for bookbinding. Apart from these enterprises there was the Islamic shareholding printing house in Sarajevo, established in 1904 with a starting capital of 75,000 crowns, the Croatian shareholding printing house, built in Mostar in 1898 with a starting capital of 25,000 crowns, and the Serbian shareholding printing house opened in Sarajevo in 1904, with a starting capital of 100,000 crowns, a printing house "*Obod*" etc. The graphic industry in Bosnia and Herzegovina employed 300 workers.

The graphic industry was oriented towards exports. Its size was in a sharp contradiction with an extremely high illiteracy rate of 88%. (Hrelja)

Construction industry

Before the occupation houses were built from wood and tile in Bosnia, and from tone in Herzegovina. After the occupation tile was replaced by bricks and shingles. Urban expansion increased demand for bricks. There were nine brick factories in Sarajevo in 1905 with an annual production of 17 million bricks. The production of bricks exceeded the absorption capacity of a domestic market. Competition among producers reduces selling price of bricks, which caused a bankruptcy of some producers. This is why the remaining producers joined together in a co-operative and agreed to reduce the output in order to stabilize the market.

August Braun established a factory of construction material in Sarajevo in 1878. The enterprise turned into a shareholding company in 1912 with a capital of 1,2 million crowns. The enterprise mainly produced tiles. The annual capacity was 7 million tiles. However, only a fraction of it was utilized. The reason for this lies in a sharp competition coming from Hungarian, Italian, Dalmatian, and Slavonian producers of materials for covering buildings.

Another company, Bihac D.D. was established in 1914 with the aim of supplying construction material for building the railway between Bosanski Brod and Bihac, with a shareholding capital of 300,000 crowns. This enterprise exploited stone from the government's quarry. The stone from this quarry was a sandy limestone, suitable for sculpture and construction works. This stone was exported to Zagreb and Vienna. The establishment employed around 820 workers.

Leather industry

Leather had been worked in Bosnia and Herzegovina before the occupation. Prior to the uprising 1875-1878 raw and tanned hides were shipped to Trieste and Vienna, making together with wool and prunes the country's most important exporting items. There were two large tanneries and numerous small establishments in Sarajevo and Mostar, while Visoko had some thirty tanneries employing three to six tanners each. They produced a large variety of leather of excellent quality together with finished and semi-cured hides. The government officials were of the opinion that the leather industry was prosperous and lucrative, and that it should be expanded. (Sugar)

Following this suggestion, the government established a large, modern tannery in Jelec. Dr Thomas Masarik, then a member of the Austrian Delegation, criticized the government for this decision, claiming that the establishment of this tannery hurt the peasantry by forcing them to skin animals according to the method demanded by the tannery. Since no other buyer was willing to purchase hides cut up in this fashion, the tannery had a virtual monopoly. Kallay defended the government's decision claiming that guaranteed purchases by the government eliminated very often fraudulent middle men. However, in-spite of elimination of the middlemen the peasantry lost the money since prices for raw hides fell while those for tanned leather rose.

The plant accumulated debts, almost exclusively owed to the government for capital, machinery and equipment, amounting to 163,120 florins. The enterprise finally failed and shut down in 1895. (Sugar)

The plant failed in spite of the fact that it had excellent conditions to be a successful business. When Alkalay and the Salom brothers bought the machinery of a dying Jelec tannery, they established a prosperous tanning company in Sarajevo.

Kallay invited Bruno Trenck, a German glove manufacturer who used 80,000 dozen hides yearly in his factories in Magdeburg and Chemnitz, to open an enterprise in Bosnia and Herzegovina. He was interested to buy three to four million marks worth of lamb, and kid skins yearly from Bosnia and Herzegovina, provided they were well cured and sorted.

Trenckmann agreed to establish the *Bosnische Feinlederfabrik* to produce and dye leather suitable for gloves, handbags, and other luxury leather products. In order to eliminate competition with the Jelec establishment it was envisaged that the Jelec factory sells all lamb and goat skins in tanned to Trenckmann at cost price, while he was to hand all the skin he had bought to

Jelec up to the quantity which would be required to keep it fully occupied.

Trenckmann was obliged to use the *Volksbank*, later the *Landesregierung bank*, and to start production at the beginning of 1894. In exchange he was assured a twenty-year monopoly, land for his factory, building material and water power free of charge. Wood for fuel was also to be supplied for free, and coal and freight would be charged at the lowest possible price. Trenckmann also received a twenty-year exemption from all taxes and duties. When everything was arranged and the factory was built in Dolac near Travnik Trenckmann changed his mind and gave up arguing that the market conditions were unfavorable and did not allow him to go ahead with starting the business. The machinery was later transferred to Sarajevo where Saloms and Alkalay used them and established the plant in Sarajevo, which employed more than twenty workers.

The leather industry, which had excellent condition for developing, failed in the same way as the textile industry, due to wrong business decisions. (Sugar)

Dynamics of sectoral and aggregate growth of manufacturing industry

The following table, provided by Palairet, is a valuable well of data which can be used to calculate an average growth rate of different sectors of the manufacturing industry and the manufacturing industry in total:

Table 15 – Bosnia and Herzegovina 1881-1915: Value-added index of a big industry (all sectors 1907 = 1000

YEAR	COAL	MINERALS	METALS	CONSTRUCTION	WOODEN MATERIAL	PAPER AND PULP	TOBACCO & FOOD	CHEMICAL PRODUCTS	ALL SECTORS
1881	2			6	2		18		29
1882	3	15		7	2		28		58
1883	5	26		7	2		28		70
1884	6	37		6	4		30	1	87
1885	8	32		7	7		31	1	89
1886	10	31		7	7		35	2	95
1887	12	28		8	11	2	37	2	105
1888	15	12		8	7	2	43	3	93
1889	17	15		9	21	2	39	2	110
1890	20	19		9	42	2	46	2	146
1891	25	22		10	37	2	50	3	155
1892	36	28		11	29	2	53	4	170
1893	46	24		13	44	2	57	4	198
1894	56	32		15	58	2	61	5	239
1895	67	40	6	21	35	2	64	28	273
1896	75	50	10	26	37	2	61	36	308
1897	77	50	22	28	33	2	66	32	324
1898	92	58	25	33	38	2	64	40	368
1899	103	63	27	36	100	2	71	59	482
1900	132	95	40	44	140	2	69	48	595
1901	149	96	49	47	152	2	68	68	659
1902	142	100	74	48	153	2	70	81	698
1903	157	81	75	57	196	2	75	73	746

1904	162	87	68	61	253	2	84	88	839
1905	181	99	61	62	256	2	84	114	895
1906	199	105	67	68	292	2	85	109	966
1907	208	103	67	76	278	23	87	118	1000
1908	221	107	71	79	285	56	85	109	1055
1909	233	87	63	84	303	69	93	125	1102
1910	237	80	71	86	280	73	92	124	1087
1911	258	85	77	91	279	83	100	113	1131
1912	286	98	83	102	288	83	108	122	1219
1913	282	126	74	103	279	82	104	115	1215
1914	270	102	62	98	173	57	118	90	1009
1915	268	87	38	93	73	20	121	65	795

SOURCE: Palairet, "Habsburg Industrial Achievement", p 142

1. Coal industry

$$(\Delta Y + Y)/Y = (1 + g)^n$$

$$282/2 = (1 + g)^{32}$$

$$141 = (1 + g)^{32} /\log$$

$$\log 141 = 32 \log (1 + g)$$

$$2.15 = 32 \log (1 + g)$$

$$\log (1 + g) = 2.15/32$$

$$\log (1 + g) = 0.067$$

$$(1 + g) = 10^{0.067}$$

$$(1 + g) = 1.166$$

$$g = 1.166 - 1$$

$$g = 0.16.6$$

$$g = 16.6\%$$

2. Minerals

$$(\Delta Y + Y)/Y = (1 + g)^n$$

$$126/15 = (1 + g)^{31}$$

$$8.4 = (1 + g)^{31} /\log$$

$$\log 8.4 = 31 \log (1 + g)$$

$$\log (1 + g) = 0.026/31$$

$$\log (1 + g) = 0.026$$

$$(1 + g) = 10^{0.026}$$

$$(1 + g) = 1.062$$

$$g = 1.062 - 1$$

$$g = 0.062$$

$$g = 6.2\%$$

3. Metal industry

$$(\Delta Y + Y)/Y = (1 + g)^n$$

$$74/6 = (1 + g)^{18}$$

$12.33 = (1 + g)^{18} /\log$

$\log 12.33 = 18 \log (1 + g)$

$\log (1 + g) = 1.10/18$

$\log (1 + g) = 0.068$

$(1 + g) = 10^{0.068}$

$(1 + g) = 1.169$

$g = 1.169 - 1$

$g = 0.16.9$

$g = 16.9\%$

4. Construction industry

$(\Delta Y + Y)/Y = (1 + g)^n$

$103/6 = (1 + g)^{32}$

$17.16 = (1 + g)^{32} /\log$

$\log 17.16 = 32 \log (1 + g)$

$\log (1 + g) = 1.23/32$

$\log (1 + g) = 0.054$

$(1 + g) = 10^{0.054}$

$(1 + g) = 1.132$

$g = 1.132 - 1$

$g = 0.132$

$g = 13.2\%$

5. Wooden materials

$(\Delta Y + Y)/Y = (1 + g)^n$

$279/2 = (1 + g)^{32}$

$139.5 = (1 + g)^{32} /\log$

$\log 139.5 = 32 \log (1 + g)$

$\log (1 + g) = 2.14/32$

$\log (1 + g) = 0.066$

$(1 + g) = 10^{0.066}$

$(1 + g) = 1.164$

$g = 1.164 - 1$

$g = 0.16.4$

$g = 16.4\%$

6. Paper and pulp

$$(\Delta Y + Y)/Y = (1 + g)^n$$

$$82/2 = (1 + g)^{27}$$

$$41 = (1 + g)^{27} /\log$$

$$\log 41 = 32 \log (1 + g)$$

$$\log (1 + g) = 1.61/27$$

$$\log (1 + g) = 0.067$$

$$(1 + g) = 10^{0.06}$$

$$(1 + g) = 1.148$$

$$g = 1.166 - 1$$

$$g = 0.14.8$$

$$g = 14.8 \%$$

7. Tobacco and food

$$(\Delta Y + Y)/Y = (1 + g)^n$$

$$82/18 = (1 + g)^{32}$$

$$4.55 = (1 + g)^{32} /\log$$

$$\log 4.55 = 32 \log (1 + g)$$

$$\log (1 + g) = 0.66 /32$$

$\log(1+g) = 0.05$

$(1+g) = 10^{0.02}$

$(1+g) = 1.047$

$g = 1.047 - 1$

$g = 0.047$

$g = 4.7\%$

8. Chemical industry

$(\Delta Y + Y)/Y = (1+g)^n$

$115/1 = (1+g)^{32}$

$115 = (1+g)^{32} /\log$

$\log 115 = 32 \log(1+g)$

$\log(1+g) = 2.06/28$

$\log(1+g) = 0.074$

$(1+g) = 10^{0.074}$

$(1+g) = 1.186$

$g = 1.186 - 1$

$g = 0.186$

$g = 18.6\%$

All sectors of manufacturing industry

$$(\Delta Y + Y)/Y = (1 + g)^n$$

$$1215/29 = (1 + g)^{32}$$

$$42 = (1 + g)^{32} / \log$$

$$\log 42 = 32 \log (1 + g)$$

$$\log (1 + g) = 1.62 / 32$$

$$\log (1 + g) = 0.051$$

$$(1 + g) = 10^{0.051}$$

$$(1 + g) = 1.1246$$

$$g = 1.1246 - 1$$

$$g = 0.1246$$

$$g = 12.46 \%$$

This is in accordance with Palairet's average annual growth rate of 12.4%, so most probably he used the data from this table.

However, it was earlier calculated that the cumulative inflation for this period was 4.4%. So, more accurately one should discount the index 1215 for the year 1913 by 1.044. A discounted index for the year 1913 is 1215/1.044, or 1164.

$$(\Delta Y + Y)/Y = (1 + g)^n$$

$$1164/29 = (1 + g)^{32}$$

$$40 = (1 + g)^{32} / \log$$

$$\log 40 = 32 \log (1 + g)$$
$$\log (1 + g) = 1.60 / 32$$
$$\log (1 + g) = 0.05$$
$$(1 + g) = 10^{0.05}$$
$$(1 + g) = 1.122$$
$$g = 1.122 - 1$$
$$g = 0.122$$
$$g = 12.2\%$$

We can use the formula to calculate how many times did the industrial production increase in this period:

$$N = 2^{na/n},$$

Where N stands for the number of times a variable increased over a period of time, na for the actual number of years, and n for the number of years in which the variable doubles.

Na is 32. We can calculate n by using a simple formula:

$$n = 72/g,$$

where n stands for the number of years in which the variable doubles, and g for the growth rate.

$$n = 72/12 = 6$$
$$N = 2^{32/6}$$
$$N = 2^{16/3}$$
$$N = 40.32$$

The industrial production increased in this period by a staggering forty times.

Evaluation

Sectoral analysis has shown huge differences in dynamics of various segments of the economy of Bosnia and Herzegovina:

Table 16 - Average annual growth rates in mining, railways, manufacturing industry, agriculture, and a foreign trade in Bosnia and Herzegovina during the Austro-Hungarian period

Sectors	Period	Average annual growth rate
Coal Industry	1881-1913	16.6%
Minerals	1881-1913	6.2%
Metal industry	1881-1913	16.9%
Construction	1881-1913	13.2%
Wood	1881-1913	16.4%
Paper and pulp	1881-1913	14.8%
Tobacco & food	1881-1913	4.7%
Chemical industry	1881-1913	18.6%
Agriculture	1878-1913	0.94% (p.c.)
Rolling stock	1900-1909	7.68%
Railway network	1900-1909	9.6%
Export of wood	1898-1911	16.6%
Foreign trade	1878-1912	6.34%
Iron	1880-1913	14.9%
Salt	1905-1913	2.3%
Manufacturing industry	1881-1913	12.1%

SOURCE: Calculated by the author (already in the chapter) using different sources.

Agriculture was the weakest sector of the Bosnian economy. Unresolved agricultural relations were a great impediment to increase in production. In addition, well-intentioned attempt to apply modern agricultural techniques did not found a fertile ground since they clashed with a culture, habits, and attitudes of the rural population. As a result, the standard of living of the peasant hardly increased.

In manufacturing industry, the government usually allowed private capitalists to set the business, and then nationalized it.

This strategy worked well in heavy industry, but was much less successful in light industry. The only bright spot in light industry was the forestry, in spite of a widespread and sharp criticism of a wanton destruction of natural resources and botched attempts of reforestation. The forestry not only provided a lion's share of government revenue, but also secured work for 20.000 employees and significantly contributed to an increase in the standard of living. Other branches of light industry were much less successful. Furthermore, many opportunities were missed where the country had excellent conditions for development. The rapid urbanization, particularly a development of Sarajevo, offered good opportunities for various industries. Yet no cement factory was built although the raw material and power was available. No furniture factory was erected, as a built up of the forestry industry. The various components which go into the manufacture of glass and pottery could be found in the country in large quantities and in excellent quality, but no glass or pottery factory was ever erected. Even brick ovens were established in insufficient numbers so that various enterprises such as the coal mines, salt springs, and iron mines at Vares had to erect their own kilns. Manufacturers and entrepreneurs addressed the unexplored possibilities and requested relevant information from the Ministry. Yet, the Ministry never responded in a positive manner, as a result of the combination of negligence and a bad planning. This factor, together with the government's unnecessary interference in the sector of the economy which should have been left to the private sector offers the explanation for the relative failure of the light industry in Bosnia and Herzegovina. (Sugar)

Overall, though, the performance of the manufacturing industry looks impressive. It grew at a staggering average annual rate of 15% during the Kallay's era, slowed down to 8.4% during the Burian's period, and only 3.3% in the last three years before the war. For the entire period an average growth rate was more than 12%. This means that the manufacturing output doubled approximately every six years. For the total period it increased by a staggering forty times.

CHAPTER SIX

ECONOMIC DEVELOPMENT OF BOSNIA AND HERZEGOVINA IN A COMPARATIVE PERSPECTIVE

Macroeconomic indicators

Comparative analysis of economic development between different countries normally includes macroeconomic indicators. Macroeconomic indicators usually follow macroeconomic objectives.

The macroeconomics objectives are goals which governments aspire to achieve. There are different classifications of macroeconomic objectives. Most commonly high growth, low unemployment, price stability, and external balances are considered major macroeconomic objectives. Sometimes, closely related to the latter stability of exchange rate is added.

It is very difficult to achieve all these objectives at the same time. This is why Paul Jacobsen, a chief executive of the International Monetary Fund in 1947, called the major macroeconomic objectives a „ magic quadrangle".

Sometimes, two more macroeconomic objectives are added to this list. They include fiscal balance, and equitable distribution of income. (Mahmutefendic)

There are difficulties in analyzing macroeconomic objectives. The first ones could be called general, and they are related to data collection. The second ones could be dubbed specific, and they are related to the fact that macroeconomic objectives had in the past different meaning and different weight compared to the modern times.

- Data collection is a very difficult operation. There are at least four problems related to data collection:
- Data collection is a very tedious, boring and expensive job. Companies try to minimize expenses and many data are lost in the process.
- Many transactions are not reported for tax purposes. Tax evasion amounts to tens of billions of dollars in most developed countries.
- Data are manipulated by companies and governments. Companies deliberately report lower revenue and higher cost and expenses so that registered profit appears lower than it is and that they pay less taxes. Also, they use so-called transfer prices, reporting higher profits in low tax rate countries and lower profits in high tax rate countries. Governments manipulate data to present economic performances better than they are. This is particularly pronounced before elections. They report higher growth rate, lower inflation and lower unemployment.
- There are sometimes errors which stem from the nature of a particular economic category. For example, somebody can be registered as unemployed and work in an informal economy. On the other hand, a wife whose husband earns a good income can decide not to work and to look after the family. She is not reported as unemployed although she is virtually without a paid job. (Mahmutefendic)
- Specific problems arise from the fact that macroeconomic objectives had different meaning and weight in the past.
  <u>Unemployment.</u> In a predominantly rural country, such as Bosnia and Herzegovina, there was overemployment in agriculture. In addition, many

works had a seasonal character, with peasants employed several months in agriculture, and the rest of a year in manufacturing industry. In such a situation it was impossible to measure unemployment rate.

Inflation. Inflation, defined as a continuous rise in an average rate of prices is relatively a new phenomenon in historical perspective. It appeared only after the WWII. Earlier in history there were episodes of a sharp rise in prices, caused by a bad harvest, wars, natural disasters, or discoveries of gold and silver mines. However, they were usually followed by periods in which a general level of prices fell, so that the overall trend was smoothed out. For example, the nineteenth century was characterized by a long-term fall in the general level of prices. One pound in 1800 was worth 93 nowadays pounds and 136 nowadays pounds in 1900. This means that the purchasing power of the pound rose in the nineteenth century. In such a situation achieving a low rate of inflation as a macroeconomic objective did not have any meaning.

External balances. In a predominantly agricultural country external balances very often depended on fluctuations in agricultural output. Achieving external balances did not have any reflection on the standard of living and a general well-being of the population. For example, in the last years of the Ottoman rule Bosnia and Herzegovina achieved a surplus in a trade balance, but the standard of living of the vast majority of people did not improve at all.

Fiscal balance. Fiscal balance, as external balances, could have fluctuated year after year. With the exception of the Kallay administration, fiscal policy was not used to promote economic growth, and in general the Keynesianism was unknown at the time. Therefore, fiscal balance had a completely different meaning and in general followed a classical economic prescription; a necessity to balance it, regardless of the impact on economic growth and the standard of living.

<u>Distribution of income</u>. The Italian statistician Conrado Gini, did his research in this field in the first decades of the twentieth century. Before him there was not a measure of distribution of income and wealth on a consistent basis. This was a middle of a so-called first Kuznets cycle, in which there were huge differences in distribution of income and wealth, without progressive taxation, which would reduce them.

In such a situation a comparative analysis of macroeconomic objectives boils down to one measure, the level of GDP. Although GDP is most often used as a measure of development it has many drawbacks:

- GDP does not comprise non- marketed activities. For example, if parents take their child to a private kindergarten they will pay for the service, which will be recorded in GDP. If they have relatives (mother, aunts) who can look after the child they will save the money. Although the same service was performed it will not be included in GDP since there was not a monetary transaction. The same applies to cleaning a flat. If we hire a professional cleaner we will need to pay for the service and this will be included in GDP. If we do it ourselves the same service will be performed by it will not be calculated as part of GDP since it is non-monetary and non-market activity. According to some estimates up to 1/3 of GDP consists of non-marketed activities.
- GDP does not comprise value created in in-formal economy. Informal economy consists of two parts; black and grey. Black economy consists of illegal activities such as drug and weapons trafficking. A larger part of informal economy comprises legal activities which are not recorded for tax purposes. For example,

if a plumber comes to our house to fix a boiler we will pay them, but they will not report it for tax purposes. The value of GDP created in informal economy varies from 10-12% in high-income countries to 50% in low-income countries. In Bosnia and Herzegovina, which is a middle-income country, GDP created in informal economy is estimated at 25%.

- GDP calculated at market exchange rate does not take into account huge differences in the level of prices in various countries. Prices are much higher in developed than in developing countries. The difference between prices of goods are smaller than the differences in prices of services. Services are much more expensive in high-income countries. This is why GDP calculated at market exchange rates gives unrealistically big differences between developed and developing countries. To rectify this international organizations have started using a concept of GDP at PPP (purchasing power parity). All prices are converted into American prices (international dollars). This measure gives a more realistic picture about differences in GDP across countries. For example, Bosnia and Herzegovina has GDP at market exchange rate of $5,000 and $12,000 at PPP.

- GDP calculated at market exchange rate does not take into account fluctuations in exchange rates. For example, the euro increased its value against the dollar from $0.84 in 2001 to $1.58 in 2008. Since the KM is pegged (fixed) to the euro a nominal GDP in Bosnia and Herzegovina doubled, although it did not affect real GDP.

- GDP does not take into account distribution of income. For example, the United States and Sweden have a similar level of GDP. However, a distribution of income is much more egalitarian in Sweden compared to the USA. This means that the standard of living of a majority of people is higher in Sweden than in the USA.

Recently, an alternative measure of development and the standard of living has been used. Human Development Index (HDI) consist of three components; 1. Income per head, 2. Level of education, which is further decomposed into a literacy level and higher education level and 3. Life expectancy. (Mahmutefendic)

In spite of the above-mentioned drawbacks, GDP per capita is still used as a main indicator of the level of development. For GDP per capita is reflected in the standard of living and is therefore considered the most relevant indicator of the level of development.

Comparison in GDP per capita between Bosnia and Herzegovina and chosen countries

Paul Welfens, suggesting strategies to boost economic growth in the Balkans after the collapse of communism, claims that the differences between the Balkan countries and the West were not that big before the World War I, when Italy, Croatia, and Bosnia and Herzegovina, were approximately at the same level of development. Their GDP per capita was at 3/5 of the German's GDP per capita, while Serbia's GDP per capita was at the half of the German's GDP per capita (Welfens)

Michael Palairet calculated GDP per capita in chosen countries and presented them in the following table:

Table17 - National product per capita in different territories in 1910 in $ in 1970

Germany	958	Bohemian lands	819
Austria	802	Hungary	616
Dalmatia	650	Italy	546
BOSNIA	546	Greece	455
Croatia	542	Transylvania	542
Serbia	462	Russia	398

SOURCE: Palairet:"Habsburg Industrial Achievement", cited from Michael Palairet:" Balkanske privrede oko 1800-1914-evolucija bez razvoja" (The Balkan Economies around 1800-1914-Evolution without Development", Cambridge University Press 1997, p 276

Palairet mentioned in the same chapter of his book that GDP per capita in Montenegro was $37 in 1910. Inflation rate in the USA was 3% on average between 1910 and 1970. To adjust the Montenegro's GDP per capita to a purchasing power of the dollar in 1970 we need to multiply 37 by $(1.03)^{60}$.

GDP (Montenegro 1910) = $37 $(1.03)^{60}$

GDP (Montenegro 1910) = $37 x 5.89

GDP (Montenegro 1910) = $ 218

On the basis of these data, it is possible to calculate indexes of GDP per capita in Bosnia and Herzegovina compared to the chosen countries.

Germany- 546/958 x 100 = 58

Austria- 546/802 x 100 = 68

Serbia -546/462 x 100 = 118

Italy – 546/546 x 100 = 100

Greece – 546/455 x 100 = 120

Russia – 546/398 = 137

Montenegro – 546/218 x 100 = 250

It is not possible to calculate index for Croatia because the data in the table are given for the Croatia proper and Slavonia, without Dalmatia and Istria.

The following table might be a useful to source for the assessment of the level of development in chosen countries across the time:

Table18 -Relative Levels of GDP per Capita

Countries Relative to the West European Average

Countries	1870	1913	1929	1950	1973	1992
West European average	100	100	100	100	100	100
UK	164	145	121	124	103	90
Ireland	89	78	66	64	60	67
Portugal	55	39	35	39	65	64
Spain	69	65	68	43	75	72
Italy	74	72	69	62	89	93
Greece	na	47	55	35	67	59
Turkey	na	28	22	24	23	25
Bulgaria	na	34	27	30	45	23
Former Yugoslavia	na	41	31	28	36	22
Romania	na	41	26	21	30	15
Czechoslovakia	59	60	70	64	60	39
Hungary	64	60	57	45	48	32
Poland			49	44	46	27
Sweden	84	89	89	122	115	97
Russia/USSR	52	43	32	51	52	27

SOURCE: Calculations based on Jackson (1982 and 1986), and Maddison (1995), in Marvin Jackson: "Intra-Balkans Trade and Economic Cooperation: Past Lessons for the Future, p 36, in George Petrakos & Stoyan Totev (editors: "The Development of the Balkan Region", Ashgate Publishing Limited, Hampshire, UK 2001

It is possible to use the figures for Greece and Italy, the two countries which appear in the both tables, to calculate the index of GDP per capita of Bosnia and Herzegovina to the Yugoslav lands.

Firstly, we will calculate the index of GDP per capita for Greece and Italy to the Yugoslav lands:

For Greece-(Index for Greece) 47/(Index for the Yugoslav lands) 41 x 100 = 115

For Italy-(Index for Italy) 72/(Index for the Yugoslav lands 41 x 100 = 175

Now, we can calculate the index of GDP per capita index for Bosnia and Herzegovina to the Yugoslav lands via Greece and via Italy:

Via Greece: 120x115/100 = 138

Via Italy: 100 x 175/100 = 175

There is a big discrepancy between the two calculations. This is why we will use the third one, which will give a more realistic outcome. Germany is not mentioned in the table. However, according to some sources (Maddison) Germany had index 109 to the West European average.

Using a figure in the first table it is possible to calculate an average GDP per capita for the West Europe:

$958/1.09 = $879

If we apply index 41 for the Yugoslav lands in the second table, we arrive at the figure of $879 x 41/100 = $360. This means that the Yugoslav lands had approximately GDP per capita $360 before the WWI.

If we divide GDP per capita in Bosnia and Herzegovina with GDP per capita for the Yugoslav lands we will get:

546/360 x 100 = 152

Therefore, index of GDP per capita in Bosnia and Herzegovina was 152 to the index of GDP per capita in the Yugoslav lands before the WWI.

Indexes of GDP per capita in Bosnia and Herzegovina and the chosen countries can be summarized in the following table:

Table19 - Indexes of GDP per capita of Bosnia and Herzegovina and the chosen countries in 1910/1913, where the latter are given index 100

Country	Index
Germany	58
Austria	68
Italy	100
Greece	120
Russia	137
Serbia	118
Montenegro	250
The Yugoslav lands	152

SOURCE: The author's calculations, based on Palairet and Jackson

According to one source (Hoare) a volume of trade in Bosnia and Herzegovina increased sevenfold during the Austro-Hungarian period. The following table, already used in the text, confirms this figure:

Table 20 - A revenue from indirect taxes in Bosnia and Herzegovina 1885 – 1913 in crowns

YEAR	INDIRECT TAXES
1885	6,226,837
1890	12,817,983
1895	16,011,791
1900	18,713,529
1905	22,791,856
1910	32,788,753
1913	43,429,483

SOURCE: Adapted from Ferdinand Hauptmann: "Austrougarska vladavina u Bosni I Hercegovini 1878-1918", str 129, u Enver Redzic (urednik): "Prilozi za istoriju Bosne i Hercegovine", ANUBiH, Sarajevo 2006

The data in the table allow the use of the formula for calculating an average growth rate of the Bosnian economy:

$$(\Delta Y + Y)/Y = (1 + g)^n.$$

$$43{,}429{,}483/6{,}226{,}837 = (1 + g)^n$$

$$6.97 = (1 + g)^n /\log$$

$$\log 6.97 = n \log (1 + g)$$

$$0.84 = 28 \log (1 + g)$$

$$\log (1 + g) = 0.84/28$$

$$\log (1 + g) = 0.03$$

$$(1 + g) = 100.03$$

$$(1 + g) = 1.071$$

$$g = 1.071 - 1$$

$$g = 0.071, \text{ or } 7.1\%$$

This result can be confirmed by the formula for sevenfold increase in any variable:

$$n = 198/g$$

$$n \times g = 198$$

$$g = 198/n$$

$$g = 198/28$$

$$g = 7.1\%$$

The following table shows a rise of population in Bosnia and Herzegovina in a period 1879-1910:

Table 21- Population in Bosnia and Herzegovina in a period 1879-1910

Year	Total population
1879	1,584,164
1885	1,336,091
1895	1,568,092
1910	1,898,044

SOURCE: Bekavac S, Skenderovic R: "Povijest 3" (History 3), Zagreb ALFA, 2009, p 238

Using these data, it is possible to calculate an average annual growth rate of population.

$$(\Delta P + P) / P = (1 + g)^n.$$

$$1.20 = (1 + g)^n / \log$$

$$\log 1.20 = 30 \log (1 + g)$$

$$0.08 = 30 \log (1 + g)$$

$$\log (1 + g) = 0.00267$$

$$(1 + g) = 10^{0.0267}$$

$$(1 + g) = 1.006$$

$$g = 1.006 - 1$$

$$g = 0.006, \text{ or } 0.6\%$$

Subtracted from 7.1%, this gives us an average annual growth rate per capita of 6.5%. This figure looks colossal, particularly when compared with most of other countries in which an average growth rate per capita ranged between 1 and 2%. However, one needs to be cautious when interpreting these data. After the occupation large chunks of the Bosnian economy were absorbed into the market. So, a good deal of the increase in GDP per capita could be explained by monetization of the activities which were previously either part of a subsistence economy, or took the form of a barter trade.

Other Indicators

The already mentioned problems in agriculture stunted its growth per capita, which amounted to less than 1% per annum on average. As a result, agricultural output per head was only at the 80% of the agricultural output per head in Serbia. (Palairet)

However, in spite of generally poor performance of domestic industrial enterprises, and insufficient conditions for take-off, to use Rostow's terminology, manufacturing industry in Bosnia and Herzegovina was far superior to the manufacturing industry in the other Balkan countries. Bosnia and Herzegovina were three times more industrialized than Serbia, and five times more industrialized than Bulgaria. With 21% of the total population of the three Balkan countries Bosnia and Herzegovina accounted for 54% of the total manufacturing industry output of the three countries.

In most other economic indicators, Bosnia and Herzegovina was more advanced than Bulgaria, Serbia, or Russia. For example, the Bosnian railways had 51 kilometers of travelers traffic in 1909. This was below the Russian standards (130 kilometers), but above the Serbian standards (45 kilometers), and the Bulgarian standards (30 kilometers). Furthermore, the Bosnian postal service delivered 16.7 letters per inhabitant in 1910, compared to 8.9 letters in Serbia, and 6.4 letters in Bulgaria. These differences were important, since the number of letters per inhabitant was in a close correlation with the GDP per capita before 1914. The Russian level was below the Bosnian level, with 12 letters per inhabitant in 1909. In foreign trade, Bosnia and Herzegovina was much more advanced compared to its Balkan neighbors.

The standard of living in a predominantly subsistence economy was difficult to measure. Nevertheless, a comparison can be made for a big industry, where data for wages are available. Average wage in 1907 was 658 crowns in 1907 in Bosnia and Herzegovina, compared to 630.5 dinars in Serbia, and 547 levs for Bulgaria (all the three currencies had the same value which was equal to the value of the French franc.) Since a daily wage in coal mining industry and a production of metal increased by 13 per in a period 1907-1910, from 2.46 crowns to 2.78 crowns between 1907 and 1910, Industrial workforce cost around 744 crowns, which was 18% more than in Serbia, and 36% more than in Bulgaria. (Palairet)

The value of exports per inhabitant was 71.4 crowns in 1910, which was 2.1 times greater than the figure for Serbia, and 2.4 times greater than the figure for Bulgaria. (Palairet)

In 1910 Bosnia and Herzegovina was somewhere between Hungary and the Balkan countries according to the level of development measured by GDP per capita. In-spite of structural problems and imbalances in economic growth the country was productive as Italy, and much more productive than Russia. Before the World War I Bosnia and Herzegovina was the most developed Balkan country, while according to the European standards belonged to middle-income countries.

CONCLUSION

The interest of Hungary and Austria, the two constituent countries of the Austro-Hungarian empire, dates back to the Middle Ages. Hungary had great aspirations on Bosnia and considered it its vassal state. The involvement of Hungary in Bosnia's affairs did not cease even after the country was conquered by Turks in 1463. Hungary tried to link up two unoccupied enclaves, the county of Jajce, and the county of Srebrenica and to create a new Bosnian kingdom under its auspice. After being decisively defeated by the Turks in the battle of Mohac in 1526, Hungarians fell under Austria, when the Austrian king Ferdinand was coronated a Hungarian king in 1527. The Austrians took over and espoused interest in liberating Bosnia from the Turks and incorporating it into its monarchy. After being defeated by the Turks in 1737 the Austrians put on hold its involvement in Bosnia's affairs for a century and a half.

A decisive event occurred in 1866, when Austria was defeated by the Prussia in the battle of Sadova/Konigratz. This excluded Austria from the German unification for good. A year later, exploiting Austria's weakness, Hungary managed to force the Austrians into the Ausgleich (Compromise), with which the Habsburg monarchy was transformed into the Austro-Hungarian empire. This revived interest of the Monarchy for Bosnia and Herzegovina. This interest came into effect in the Congress of Berlin in 1878, when the great powers decided that the Austro-Hungarian empire occupies Bosnia and Herzegovina and introduce its administration to the country.

At the time of the Berlin Congress, Bosnia was almost as backward as some African colonies after two centuries of Turkish inertia and misrule. Roads were in appalling condition and were in a worse state than in the medieval period. The main transport means was still a horse. There was only one railway line, connecting Banjaluka to Dobrljin, on the Croatian border. In a predominantly subsistence economy internal trade was undeveloped. External trade was more developed and 1865 Bosnia recorded a surplus in trade balance. Financial institutions were rudimentary. The main one was Menafi-Sanduk, the outdated remnant of the old days. Those who needed money had to turn to private lenders and to loan sharks, who charged exorbitant interests.

More than 90% of the population was employed in agriculture. There was a small number of the peasants who own the land. The majority were employed as serfs, landless peasants, who had to pay one third of their yield to the landowner and one tenth (tithe) to the state. However, corrupt and greedy tax collectors would usually turn a tithe into 20% tax. The peasants had to sell their crops at unfavorable time, to pay off debts to loan sharks, and to pay a tithe and one third to the landowner. In practice they were left with only 35% of the value of their crops. In such a situation the peasants were not motivated to increase production since a lion share of an increase in yield would go to the state, loan sharks, and landowners.

Cattle breading was in a much better situation, since it was not subject to the tithe and one third paid to the landowner, since pastures were free for use.

Christian Orthodox peasants, who made up the largest percentage of serfs, hoped that the new Christian power would expropriate landowners and give them out the land in a way it was done in France after the Revolution. This did not happen for three reasons. Firstly, the law of 22 February 1880 stated that all revenues for economic development of Bosnia and Herzegovina must be collected in the country. The tithe was a very important source of income for the government. Secondly, the new authorities were aware that they had support of Catholics, but that a vast majority of Christian Orthodox were not loyal to them. The agrarian reform would alienate Muslims, which they did not want to happen. In addition, not being accustomed to any work, Muslim landowners would impoverish, which would be an additional burden to the state. Thirdly, every law concerning Bosnia and Herzegovina had to be passed in both Hungarian and Austrian Parliament. The powerful Hungarian landowners, who dominated the Hungarian Parliament, would oppose the land reform in Bosnia and Herzegovina, fearing that it could be a "bad example" for Hungary. Instead of land reform the government started giving the peasants loans and credits to buy off the land. Before the war, around 40% of the peasants bought the land from their previous masters.

However, this did not improve the situation in agriculture since new land owners lacked the working capital. Also, neither the big landowners nor the landless peasants had an incentive to increase production. In addition, well-intentioned modern methods introduced by the government fell on the unfertile soil since they were incompatible with the culture of the local population. As a result, agriculture in Bosnia and Herzegovina was far less developed than in Serbia and Bulgaria.

The government gave priority to the development of manufacturing industry. Bosnia and Herzegovina had huge natural resources for the development of various sectors of heavy and light industry. The government unwittingly applied a set of economic doctrines in its industrial policy, some of which did not exist at the time. They included Mercantilism, to a certain extent the List's concept of educational tariffs, the Lewis' concept of a dual economy, the H-O-S theory, the inverse Hoffman model, the Soviet/Nazi planned economy and the Keynesian deficit financing.

The manufacturing industry was mainly located near the sources of raw materials and close to transport infrastructure. The government would usually allow private businesses to set up and after several years it would nationalize them. This worked well in transport industry and heavy industry, but not as well in light industry with the exception of forestry, which grew at staggering double-digit growth rates and became a dangerous competitor in the world market (die Bosnische Gefahr).

The assessment of economic development in Bosnia and Herzegovina can be conducted on two levels - the sectoral one, and the aggregate one.

On the sectoral level the criticism of the economic policy could be pointed in the following directions:

- Neglect of agriculture, which resembles the Soviet model. As a result, comparative advantages for development of food processing industry were missed.
- Unbalanced regional growth. Building industrial capacities near the sources of raw materials and close to transport links left large areas of Herzegovina and Eastern Bosnia unindustrialized and unconnected with transport network.
- Unbalanced sectoral growth. Heavy industry grew at double-digit rates, while many sectors of light industry showed a poor performance.
- Unbalanced involvement of foreign and domestic capital. A predominance of foreign capital did not create conditions for a self-sustained growth. As a result, Bosnia and Herzegovina failed to enter the Rostow's stage of take-off.

On the aggregate level, however, the results were impressive. The manufacturing industry grew at an average annual rate of more than 12% in a period 1881-1913. This growth was largest during Kallay's administration when manufacturing industry grew at an average rate of 15%. In 1907 Bosnia and Herzegovina was three times more industrialized than Serbia and five times more industrialized than Bulgaria. This was reflected in an increase in GDP per capita. Before the WWI Bosnia and Herzegovina was more developed than Russia, Greece, and Serbia. It was at the same level of development as the Croatia proper with Slavonia and Italy. Its GDP per capita was roughly at the 3/5 of the GDP per capita in Germany and 2/3 of the GDP per capita in Austria.

However, in spite of the generally poor performance of domestic industrial enterprises, and insufficient conditions for take-off, to use Rostow's terminology, manufacturing industry in Bosnia and Herzegovina was far superior to the manufacturing industry in the other Balkan countries. Bosnia and Herzegovina were three times more industrialized than Serbia, and five times more industrialized than Bulgaria. With 21% of the total population of the three Balkan countries Bosnia and Herzegovina accounted for 54% of the total manufacturing industry output of the three countries.

In most of other economic indicators, Bosnia and Herzegovina was more advanced than Bulgaria, Serbia, or Russia. For example, the Bosnian railways had 51 kilometers of travelers traffic in 1909. This was below the Russian standards (130 kilometers), but above the Serbian standards (45 kilometers), and the Bulgarian standards (30 kilometers). Furthermore, the Bosnian postal service delivered 16.7 letters per inhabitant in 1910, compared to 8.9 letters in Serbia, and 6.4 letters in Bulgaria. These differences were important, since the number of letters per inhabitant was in a close correlation with the GDP per capita before 1914. The Russian level was below the Bosnian level, with 12 letters per inhabitant in 1909. In foreign trade, Bosnia and Herzegovina was much more advanced compared to its Balkan neighbors.

The standard of living in a predominantly subsistence economy was difficult to measure. Nevertheless, a comparison can be made for a big industry, where data for wages are available. Average wage in 1907 was 658 crowns in 1907 in Bosnia and Herzegovina, compared to 630.5 dinars in Serbia, and 547 levs for Bulgaria (all the three currencies had the same value which was equal to the value of the French franc.) Since a daily wage in coal mining industry and a production of metal increased by

13 per in a period 1907-1910, from 2.46 crowns to 2.78 crowns between 1907 and 1910, Industrial workforce cost around 744 crowns, which was 18% more than in Serbia, and 36% more than in Bulgaria. (Palairet)

The value of exports per inhabitant was 71.4 crowns in 1910, which was 2.1 times greater than the figure for Serbia, and 2.4 times greater than the figure for Bulgaria. (Palairet)

In a nutshell, before World War I Bosnia and Herzegovina was the most developed Balkan country and in European relations it was a middle-income country.

APPENDIX ONE – SEVEN DECADES OF "FREEDOM"

The First Yugoslavia. WWI brought tens of millions of deaths, material devastation, and the complete change of the political map of the world. Four great empires, namely the German, the Austro-Hungarian, The Russia, and the Turkish, disappeared and several new states were created in Europe, including Yugoslavia. Yugoslavia was carved out from the remnants of the two empires, the Ottoman, and the Austro-Hungarian, populated with the South Slavs. The country was a mosaic of different religions, ethnicities, races and cultures, deeply divided by history, and united only by the one thing, belonging to the same race which was endangered by disgruntled, rapacious, and vengeful neighbors. In 1918 Bosnia and Herzegovina was incorporated into the new state. Its position significantly deteriorated compared to the previous period. There were two sets of factors, objective, and subjective, which contributed to this.

Objective factors. Objective factors could be divided into two groups, internal and external.

a) Internal factors. Yugoslavia was one of the most complex independent states in the world. The firs constitution, the *Vidovdan* constitution, (the St Vitus Day constitution) was democratic on paper, and to certain extent even social-democratic. However, after the communist worker Alija Alijagic assassinated Milorad Draskovic, the minister of interior in 1921, the Communist party was outlawed. In the interwar period the strength of Communist party was a measure of democracy. One of the reasons why Czechoslovakia was considered a highly democratic country was that it had a strong communist party. In the Balkan countries, with fragile democracies, communist parties were banned. An additional blow to democracy was delivered by the king Alexander, who abolished the constitution in 1929, banned all the political parties, and established a personal dictatorship.

The main political disputes occurred between the Serbs and the Croats, the two most numerous ethic groups. The Serbs wanted a unitary and centralized state, while the Croats were in favor of a decentralized and federalized state. Only three ethnic groups were recognized by the constitution, the Serbs, the Croats, and the Slovenes. The Macedonians were treated as Sothern Serbs, and their language was banned from the official use. Montenegrins were not recognized as well. They were treated as Serbs, and their Church was abolished, with its property being appropriated by the Serbian Orthodox Church. Slavic Muslims were treated as Serbs and the Croats of the Islamic faith. A lack of recognition means by definition a status of second-class citizens. In 1939 the Banovina Hrvatska (the Croatian dukedom) was created without federalizing the rest of the state. This appeased the Croats to a certain extent but enraged the Serbs who lived in the Croatian Banovina. It seems that only the Slovenes were happy with political arrangements in the state since most of them lived in the compact territory of the *Dravska Banovina*. It seems that Yugoslavia was proving the accuracy of the John Stuart Mill's statement that democracy was next to impossible in multiethnic states.

External circumstances. External circumstances could be divided into two groups, political, and economic.

a) Political circumstances. The Treaty of Versailles punished defeated nations by drawing borders which cut into tissues of different ethnic groups, leaving many of them minorities in the newly created states. For example, the state of Czechoslovakia had two constituent ethnic groups, the Czechs, and the Slovaks, although the German national minority outnumbered the Slovaks. Yugoslavia accommodated large numbers of Albanians, Hungarians,

Germans, and Italians. Their respective states wanted redrawing of the borders. The situation aggravated for Yugoslavia after the Fascists Conquest of power in Italy, the Nazi ascent to power in Germany, and particularly after the assassination of the king Alexander in Marseille in 1934. The country had to take loans abroad to beef up its army and to protect its fragile and precarious position.

b) Economic circumstances. In the interwar period the world economy did not perform well. For example, from 1913 to 1939 the world trade grew at an average annual rate of 0.4%, compared to 7.3% in the decades after the WWII. Using the terminology of the long wave theories the world economy was stuck in a downward phase of the third Kondratieff. This was the period in which the UK was not able, and the USA was not willing to assume a leadership in the world economy.

The gold standard which functioned smoothly from 1870 until 1914 was suspended with the outbreak of WWI. After the war the gold standard was temporarily resumed, which led to a stabilization of capitalism from 1925 until 1929. But even in this period the Yugoslav economy did not perform well. According to some sources (Jackson), the Yugoslav index of GDP per capita to the Western European average fell from 41% in 1913 to 31% in 1929. The Great Depression struck the most agricultural countries, since their terms of trade significantly deteriorated. With the exception of Slovenia, which had a soft landing, many other parts of Yugoslavia, including Bosnia and Herzegovina, recorded a fall in GDP from 1929 to 1938. In addition, Bosnia and Herzegovina had the highest birth rate in the whole of Yugoslavia.

c) Subjective factors. Mehmed Spaho, the leader of the JMO (the Yugoslav Muslim Organization), struck a deal with the ruling Radical and Democratic party. He would vote for the *Vidovdan* constitution, provided that it contained the clause 135, which guarantees administrative borders of Bosnia and Herzegovina. But even this concession did not help much Bosnia and Herzegovina, as testified by Nikola Mandic, the Bosnian Croat politician:

"Before unification I could not imagine our unification in that way, in which Belgrade would be in unification everything, and Zagreb, Ljubljana, Sarajevo and Split only diminutive market-towns of fragmented self-governing units …. I am happy that Belgrade is growing, but I am sorry to see that at the same time, for example, Sarajevo is falling". (Nikola Mandic, speech at the Yugoslav parliament session of 26 June 1922), (Hoare)

The submersion of Bosnia and Herzegovina in a larger, unitary state, dominated by Serbia and Serbia's conflict with the Croatian national movement disrupted a delicate balance which existed between the three main ethnic groups during the Austro-Hungarian period. The Bosnian politicians became disoriented, with a low self-esteem, feeling that the destiny of the country was increasingly decided by Belgrade and Zagreb, without any considerations for Bosnia-Herzegovina needs and traditions.

Nikola Mandic denounced the stagnation of Bosnia and Herzegovina's economy, depletion of its finances and atrophy of its administration under a Serbian-dominated government in his speech in the already mentioned session of the Yugoslav parliament. In his view Bosnia-Herzegovina prosperity could only be achieved by the return of political autonomy: "*Bosnia and Herzegovina has been brought directly to the verge of collapse. And we Bosnians and Herzegovinians, particularly Croats and Muslims, are concerned that the only way out of this intolerable state is that, through autonomy according to state right, our state administration be decentralized; i.e. that Bosnia and Herzegovina receive its provincial parliament with legislative powers for provincial requirements, with its own budget and provincial government which would be responsible to the parliament for its administration, while the country would be bound to make its contribution for the common affairs of state according to its fiscal strength".* (Hoare)

In 1929 the kingdom of Serbs, Croats and Slovenes was renamed to the kingdom of Yugoslavia. The state was divided into nine provinces. Serbs did well for themselves. With only 39% of the population of the country they acquired majority in six provinces; i.e. on the 66% of the Yugoslav territory. Croats got only two provinces with their majority, Montenegrins one, while Muslims, who lived in four provinces made up majority nowhere. This meant a partition of Bosnia and Herzegovina into four provinces. "The icing on the cake" occurred in 1939, when a further division of Bosnia and Herzegovina occurred after the establishment of the Croatian dukedom. All these political and legal changes contributed to a worsening political, cultural, and economic situation in Bosnia and Herzegovina. This was succinctly expressed in individual and collective statements issued by the Bosnian communist politicians.

Djuro Pucar stated: "The peoples of Bosnia and Herzegovina aspired, too, from earlier times, for freedom and democracy. These aspirations could not be achieved in the former Yugoslavia, in which Bosnia and Herzegovina was a semi colony, and as such, oppressed by the Great Serbian regime and by other reactionaries" (Hoare).

Rodoljub Colakovic, the prominent Bosnian Serb communist politician, who was born in a town of Bijeljina, on the border between Bosnia and Serbia, talked about the love he felt for Serbia in his early youth, and the sadness which engulfed when Serbia was temporarily occupied by the Austro-Hungarian,

German, and Bulgarian army during the WWI. After the war, his love for Serbia subsided, and he became increasingly disillusioned with the way the new state was functioning: "From Serbia to Bosnia came various people: bureaucrats, sabre-wielders, petty politicians. Regardless of their occupation, almost all of them had in themselves something irascible and policemen-like and behaved in Bosnia, which yearned for freedom and justice, like conquerors. Consequently, my love for Serbia cooled and from my homeland, where those people who in the name of Serbia ruled Bosnia had already begun to persecute me, I no longer looked with rapture upon the blue mountains of Serbia". (Hoare)

The Bosnian communist youth, students at the Belgrade and Zagreb university, raised thei voice in a favor of the autonomy for Bosnia and Herzegovina. They circulated a petition in December 1939 among Bosnian students at the two universities. Entitled "Against War! For Freedom, Democracy and Equality of Nations! For the autonomy of Bosnia and Herzegovina!" and signed "Bosnian-Herzegovinian Student Youth ", it was directed against the partition of the country according to the *Sporazum* between Cvetkovic and Macek, as well as against the Serb-nationalist opposition to Bosnian autonomy.

The petition condemned the Serb elements, who were against the autonomy, and who have arisen in defense of their lucrative positions and those who for twenty years plundered and terrorized Bosnia and Herzegovina. The petition linked the campaign for Bosnian autonomy for improved living conditions for Bosnian people, who were living in black misery and poverty, ruled by ignorance and illiteracy and prey to tuberculosis and syphilis despite the country's enormous riches in form of forests, mines, cattle, fruit, vegetables and tobacco. (Hoare).

The Yugoslav economy grew at an average annual rate of 1.7% per capita in the interwar period. (Gligorov) If we apply our formula:
1.7 x 22 x 100/72,

We will arrive at the figure of 52%. This means that the Yugoslav economy before the WWII reached the level of development of Bosnia and Herzegovina before the WWI. Since the Bosnian economy contracted in this period its GDP per capita fell below the Yugoslav average; 86% in 1947 (Hoare), and 79% in 1953 (Domljan).

The Second Yugoslavia. The AVNOJ (Antifascist Council of National Liberation of Yugoslavia) decided on 29th November 1943 that the new state of Yugoslavia would be organized as a federation, consisting of six republics; Slovenia, Croatia, Bosnia and Herzegovina, Serbia, Montenegro, and Macedonia. A prominent Bosnian politician Dusko Sakota, described the new federal arrangement of Yugoslavia in the following way: "Our federation was established in order to resolve the national question. Thus, that the principle of the Federation has been consistently realized is manifest in the fact that the People's Republics are sovereign states. They are limited only in the right that the peoples of Yugoslavia have, through their own decision, transferred to the Federal People's Republic of Yugoslavia. The transfer of these rights was necessary to achieve economic and political co-operation and the reciprocal assistance of the people's republics; their common defense, state security and independence; and with the goal of a unified democratic manner of the state and social order of all the People's Republics in the composition of the FNRJ. Other than these most important affairs of importance to all the peoples, exercised through the Federal government in the general interest, the People's Republics exercise their government independently maintaining their sovereignty". (Hoare- The Bosnian Muslims in the World War II)

This would imply a great deal of freedom and independence for the republics in running their own affairs. In practice, though, Yugoslavia was a centralized federation until 1974. This had negative consequences for the development of Bosnia and Herzegovina. Firstly, its status as regards the level of development was uncertain. According to the level of industrialization (the legacy of the Austro-Hungarian period), Bosnia and Herzegovina should have been classified as a developed republic. According to the level of GDP per capita (the legacy of the Kingdom of Yugoslavia) Bosnia and Herzegovina should have been classified as underdeveloped republic.

It was decided by the central authorities that Bosnia and Herzegovina should be a supplier of the goods of base and extractive industry; i.e. raw materials and semi-finished products. This was the case even hen there were excellent conditions to develop enterprise which would produce final products (abundance of raw materials, closeness to transport infrastructure, required technology and qualified workforce. Illustrative example, unfortunately one of the many, with a soda factory in Lukavac. Technologists, geologists, and economists gave a "go ahead" to the new factory, claiming in their report that it had excellent conditions to achieve technological, productive, and allocative efficiency. In-spite of this, under the pressure of politics, it was decided that the necessary raw materials such as salt and quartz would be supplied to a soda factory in Pancevo in Vojvodina. (Hodzic)

The problem with this concept was that the prices of raw materials were fixed, while those of final products rose, since they were formed freely in the Yugoslav market. This produced a transfer of value from Bosnia and Herzegovina to already more developed republics and autonomous province of Vojvodina.

Because of this Bosnia and Herzegovina had the lowest annual growth rate of GDP per capita in a period 1952-68, which amounted to 4.2%. As a result, the index of GDP per capita to the Yugoslav average fell from 86% in 1947 to 69% in 1965 and to 64% in 1978. (Hoare)

Angus Maddison estimates that the Yugoslav economy grew at an average annual rate of 4.49% per capita in a period 1950-73. (Maddison)This means that the Bosnian economy grew at the rate of almost 0.3% lower per annum compared to the Yugoslav average. If we apply our formula

0.3 x 16 x 100/72,

We will arrive at the figure of around 6.5. This means that the index of Bosnia GDP per capita fell by 6.5% to the Yugoslav average in the most successful period of the Yugoslav economy.

The economic neglect by the Yugoslav center resembled the same attitude of Bosnia and Herzegovina by the Yugoslav kingdom in the interwar period. The Communist regime failed to keep its promises to eradicate inequality and discrimination among the Yugoslav peoples and republics, instead maintaining them subordinated to Belgrade. The changes which occurred in the late 1960s led to improvement in economic performance of the Bosnian economy. In 1965 the Federal Parliament established the Federal Fund for the Accelerated Development of the Underdeveloped Republics and Kosovo. Bosnia and Herzegovina was classified as an underdeveloped republic, and was entitled to receive aid from the Fund. In a period 1976-1980 the Bosnian economy grew at a higher rate than the Yugoslav economy. This led to a minor increase in the GDP per capita index compared to the Yugoslav average. (Hoare) Census in 1981 showed that Bosnia and Herzegovina accounted for 18.8% of the population of Yugoslavia and 12.2% of the Yugoslav social product (a measure similar to GDP and used in the socialist countries). (Ramet). This means that the GDP per capita index slightly increased to 66% of the Yugoslav average. During the 1980s when Yugoslavia went through a deep economic and political crisis, which eventually resulted in its demise, the index remained the same in-spite of the losses incurred by a financial scandal related to the *Agrokomerc* enterprise.

The following data, provided by Maddison, can shed a light on comparative economic development of Bosnia and Herzegovina before the break-up of Yugoslavia:

TABLE 22 - GDP Per Capita in Successor States of Former USSR in 1990 (1990 international dollars)

REPUBLIC	GDP per capita
Belarus	7153
Estonia	10733
Latvia	9841
Lithuania	8591
Moldova	6211
Ukraine	5995
Russian Federation	7762

SOURCE: Angus Maddison, op.cit, p341

TABLE 23 – GDP Per Capita in Successor Republics of Former Yugoslavia in 1990 (1990 international dollars)

REPUBLIC	GDP per capita
Bosnia	3791
Croatia	6971
Macedonia	3641
Slovenia	10982
Serbia-Montenegro	5282

SOURCE: Angus Maddison, op.cit, p 338

TABLE 24 – Levels of Per capita GDP in European Countries, Annual Estimates for 1990 (1990 international dollars)

COUNTRY	GDP per capita
Austria	16,881
Belgium	17,194
Denmark	18,463
Finland	16,868
France	18,093
Germany	15,932
Italy	16,320
Greece	9,984

SOURCE: Angus Maddison, op.cit, p 276 & 277

From the data in the tables, it is possible to calculate GDP per capita index for Bosnia and Herzegovina to the chosen countries:

Russia – 3791/7762 x 100 = 49

Greece – 3791/9984 x 100 = 38

Italy – 3791/16320 x 100 = 23

Germany – 3791/15932 x 100 = 24

Austria – 3791/16881 x 100 = 22

Serbia- 3791/5282 x 100 = 72

Yugoslavia – 3791/5696 x 100 = 66

These indices can be combined in one table with the indices for 1910/1913:

TABLE 25 - GDP per capita index for Bosnia and Herzegovina for 1910/1913 and 1990 compared to the chosen countries where the latter are given index 100

COUNTRY	1910/1913	1990
Russia	137	49
Greece	120	38
Italy	100	23
Germany	58	24
Austria	67	22
Serbia	118	72
Yugoslav lands/Yugoslavia	152	66

SOURCE: The author's calculations based on Palairet, Maddison and Jakcson

SAPIENTI SAT!! The data in the table show that the Bosnia and Herzegovina's Road from "slavery" to "freedom" proved to be a disaster.

APPENDIX TWO – ASSESSMENT OF YUGOSLAVIA

Yugoslavia can be assessed on three different levels, against three criteria; political, economic, and cultural.

Political assessment of Yugoslavia. The nineteen century was characterized by the rise in romantic national sentiments as a predecessor of the creation of the nation states. As in other Central European nations the bearers of national ideas, whether Croatian or Yugoslav, were in Croatia students, intellectuals and a small but active middle class. The first national idea to emerge in the 1820s was the Illyrian movement, named after the Illyrians, the ancient tribe. The South Slav thinkers thought that this was the most appropriate name for the movement since they assumed that the Illyrians were their ancestors. The main figure of the movement was Ljudevit Gaj. A close adherent of the romantic national currents so strong in Europe of this time, Gaj was influenced by the Slavic scholars and writers such as P.J. Safari, Jan Kollar, and J. Dobrovsky. Gaj got his chance in 1835 when he obtained permission from the Habsburg authorities to publish a Croatian newspaper, Danica (Morning Star). The Austrian government wanted to strengthen Croatian opposition to the growing and aggressive Hungarian nationalism.

Gaj advocated linguistic, cultural, and political unity of the empire of South Slavs. The main practical aim of the movement was to bridge the gap between various South Slav ethnicities and to create a bulwark against Hungarian influence. From 1835 there was an explosion of literary activity and publications in this direction. Gaj persuaded Croatian writers to use *Stokavian* rather than the *Kajkavian* dialect in order to create a common literary language as a basis of political co-operation.

The Illyrian movement enjoyed a great popularity among Croatian intellectuals, but the Slovenes and Serbs were not receptive to its ideas. The Slovenes were not threatened by the

Hungarians and were the most loyal to the Habsburg dynasty. In addition, the Slovenian language was of the same origin, but distinct from the language which Croats and Serbs used. Slovenes wanted cultural and linguistic autonomy within the empire. Most Serbian leaders at this time followed the ideas espoused in *Nacertanije* of Ilija Garasanin and were in favor of the creation of the Greater Serbia, which would comprise all the territories were the Serbs made up majority of population. Vuk Karadic was unsympathetic to the idea, claiming that all South Slavs were Serbs of the three faiths. Most Serb intellectuals in Vojvodina were against the movement. (Yelavich)

In-spite of its limitations the movement was considered a threat to Hungarian and Austrian authorities. They tried to control publications, fearing that the spread of the movement's ideas might be the part of a wider Pan-Slavic movement.

The union between the Serbs and Croats strengthen during the revolution in 1848. Josip Jelacic, the colonel in the Austrian army and the ban of Croatia, wanted freedom from Hungarian administrative control, a separate parliament, the abolition of serfdom, and the restoration of the Triune Kingdom, that is, the union of Croatia, Dalmatia, and Slavonia. Of these historical Croatian lands Austria ruled Dalmatia, while Hungary controlled Croatia and Slavonia. When Kossuth rejected these demands outright, the Croatians turned to Vienna.

At this time the Croatian leaders found an ally in the Serbs of Vojvodina, who also sought local self-government and were willing to unite with the Croats in a common state. Both Serbs and Croats joined the Serbian volunteers from the principality, now fought together against the Hungarians. (Yelavich)

Although both the Serbs and Croatians were strongly anti-Hungarian, neither at this time opposed the Habsburg government. In 1848 their ideas were best expressed in the Austro-Slav program, whose purpose was to gain political equality for the Slavs within a federalized empire. In 1849

Serbian and Croatian military units actively participated in crushing the Hungarian revolution.

The revolution of 1848-49 marked the end of the Illyrian movement. In the following decade two opposing political movements emerged. The first, whose founders were Ante Starcevic and Eugen Kvaternik, was an extreme Croatian nationalist movement. Its aim was the establishment of an independent Greater Croatia. Thy considered both Hungarians and Germans enemies. Also, they were against the accommodation with the Serbs and Slovenes, considering the Serbs as Croats of the Christian Orthodox faith, and Slovenes as mountainous Croats.

The Illyrian tradition was carried on by the Catholic clerics Josip Juraj Strossmayer and Franjo Racki. Strossmayer, the bishop of Djakovo and Croatia's leading ecclesiastical spokesman, as an experienced and astute politician with great influence and authority among his own people and abroad. Canon Racki, on the other hand, was more of intellectual and theoretician. He developed the basic ideas of Yugoslavism, as the new movement was named. The difference between Illyrianism and Yugoslavism was that the former movement was concerned with unification of the South Slavs of the empire and Trialism, i.e. a transformation of the empire into Austro-Hungarian-Slavic monarchy, which would be organized as a federal state, while Yugoslavism aimed at the unification of all the South Slavs including those in the Balkan countries. To further their goals Strossmayer and Racki established a in Zagreb a "Yugoslav" rather than a "Croatian" Academy of Sciences and Arts, to provide an outlet for all South Slavic scholarly publications. (Yelavich)

In line with his beliefs, Strossmayer attempted to establish contacts with the Serbian government. Prince Michael and his minister of interior Garasanin accepted the offer. However, they wanted to use Stroassmayer for their goal, which was to gather Montenegro, Greece, and Romania in a coalition against the

Ottoman empire. Their target was Turkey, not the Habsburg Monarchy. When Strossmayer hoped that he reached the agreement with the Serbian government, Belgrade negotiated an agreement with Hungarians at the expense of the Croats. (Yelavich)

Apparently, Strossmayer was betting for the wrong horse. The Obrenovic dynasty led the Austrophile foreign policy, and was never interested in a destiny of the South Slavs in the Habsburg empire. In addition, there were two occurrences which drove a wedge between the Serbs and Croats. The first one was a quarter of a century dispute over Bosnia and Herzegovina. The second one was the new Croatian ban Khuen Hedervary's divide and rule policy. He favored the Serbian minority in educational, economic, and political matters, gaining the support of the Serbian middle class, some intellectuals and the clergy. Understandably, the Croats increasingly offered their support to the Croatian Party of Rights, established by Ante Starcevic and Eugen Kvaternik. In the 1890s relations were so bad that bloody clashes took place between Croats and Serbs in Zagreb and other cities. These incidents generated an angry response from Belgrade where some radical elements went so far to demand a war of extermination between the two South Slav peoples. (Yelavich)

A decisive turnover in the Serbian foreign policy came in 1903, when military coup d'état overthrew the Obrenovic dynasty and brought the Karadjordjevic dynasty into power. King Peter had ambitions to expand Serbia to the West and to the South and to create either the Greater Serbia, or a wider South Slav state. During his reign, Serbia was almost constantly in conflict with her northern neighbor. This conflict culminated in a so called "Customs union war" in 1906. In a new political environment, it was natural that Belgrade should become a cultural and intellectual center for South Slav activities. There were congresses of students, teachers, and physicians as well as art exhibition and concerts. In 1904 some students and intellectuals formed a society called Slovenski Jug (the Slavic South), whose purpose was to bring about the unity of not only Serbs, Croats, and Slovenes, but also the Bulgars, after the improvement in relations between Belgrade and Sofia. Serbia under the Karadjordjevic dynasty was now a point of attraction. (Yelavic)

Changes were also taking place in Croatia. The Hungarian pressure against the Croatians had led them to emphasize their own national idea and not Yugoslavism. However, after 1895, following student disorders in Zagreb, many South Slav students left to study in Prague. There they came under the influence of Professor Thomas Masaryk, who along with Strossmayer, became a foremost advocate of the Yugoslav idea. Masaryk wanted to persuade his Serb and Croat students to stick together and to repudiate the Hungarian and Austrian "divide and conquer" policy, aimed at driving a wedge between the Serbs and Croats, and maintaining the dual system. Masaryk's advice was taken aboard. By 1903 a new generation of young Serbs and Croats existed who were determined to work together. They held meetings and attended congresses in Belgrade. (Yelavich)

At the same time co-operation between the Serbs and Croats was strengthen in Dalmatia. Croatian and Serbian politicians usually co-operated except when their aims diverged such as regards Bosnia and Herzegovina. Croatian politicians wanted to capitalize of drift between the Hungarians and Austrians regarding the common army. They were willing to co-operate with the Hungarians, and even Italians, since they considered Vienna the biggest threat to their aim of establishing the Triune Kingdom. As a result of this the Rijeka (Fiume) Resolution of 1905 was passed by a meeting of the Croatian parties of Dalmatia. Two weeks later at Zadar (Zara) the Serbian parties of the entire empire endorsed this plan provided that the Serb nationality was recognized in the Triune Lands. This in turn led to then formation of the Croatian-Serbia Coalition of 1905, whose program was based on the Rijeka and Zadar resolutions and whose membership was drawn from both parts of the Monarchy. The goal of the Coalition was to achieve the South

Slav unity within the empire to be followed in a future by the union of all Yugoslavs. The coalition, reflecting the complexity of the political situation I Croatian lands, was surprisingly composed of the Croatian Party of Rights, the Croatian Progressive party, the Serbian Independent party, the Social Democrats, and prominent non-party figures. The leadership lay in the hands of Frano Supilo, Ante Trumbic, Josip Smodlaka, and Svetozar Pribicevic, all of whom were to play important roles in the future Yugoslav politics. (Yelavich)

Uncompromising Hungarian policy and its reconciliation with Vienna pushed the coalition closer to Serbia. Many of the ties with Belgrade remained secret but the coalition did not conceal its desire for South Slav unity. In addition, the coalition won the majority in the Croatian Sabor in elections in 1906 and 1908. Although the coalition did not represent the majority of the population in Croatia it nevertheless managed to create a strong front in its struggle for the unification of South Slavs.

In spite of these successes of the coalition, the vast majority of the Croats wanted a reform within the empire, not the union with Serbia. The Pure Party of Rights, which separated from the Croatian Party of Rights in 1890s, was espousing the idea of the Greater Croatia, which will include Bosnia and Herzegovina, and which will remain in the empire. This viewpoint was shared with the Social Democrats. The Pure Party of Rights could not hide its hostility towards the Serbs, and did not want any union with Serbia for two reasons; firstly, awareness of religious differences, and secondly, awareness of cultural backwardness of Serbia. The Croatian Peasants' Party of Stjepan Radic, which was to become the major Croatian political party after the creation of Yugoslavia, was of the similar opinion.

Majority of Croats were joined in their attitude by the Slovenes. The two major Slovenian parties, the Clerical Party, and the Slovene Liberal Party, were interested in gaining more autonomy for Slovenia, but within the empire and not at its expense. In the same manner the Social Democrats stressed national autonomy in cultural affairs, not the break-up of the Monarchy. Only some students of the *Preporod* (Renaissance) group, founded during the Balkan Wars, believe that the Slovene national question could be solved within the framework of a larger South Slav state. Yugoslavism, thus, was only a minor political force among the Slovenes before 1914. (Yelavich)

Enthusiasm in Serbia for the overall Yugoslav idea was even more lukewarm than in Slovenia. The dominant political forces in the country, the army officers and the politicians, were not so concerned with the fate of the South Slavs of a dual monarchy but more to the Serbs who lived in Bosnia and Herzegovina and Croatia. Therefore, they aimed at the unification of all the Serbian lands rather than the creation of a larger South Slav state.

The Serbian Prime Minister Nikola Pasic, of the Radical party, was faced with two alternative roads-whether Serbia should concentrate on the establishment of the Greater Serbia or seek a united South Slav state. There was no doubt that the Serbian idea had an overwhelming support of the Serbian people-the politicians, professional men, soldiers, clergy, peasants, and even most of the students and intellectuals. Pasic himself adhered to this view. Furthermore, Serbian nationalism was in tradition of the past while Yugoslavism was at best a nebulous concept.

At the same time, Pasic recognized that he could not rebuff the supporters of the Yugoslav idea. He expected the state of enmity with the Dual Monarchy to continue in the future. Unliberated Serbian lands lay within that state. Therefore, any individuals or group that could aid in the Serbian objectives was a welcomed ally. The Serbian government secretly maintained relations not only with the Serbs, but also with the Yugoslav sympathizers in Bosnia and Herzegovina, Vojvodina, and Croatia, lands with large Serb population. Pasic did not espouse any interest in Slovenes, and was well, aware that the advocates of the Yugoslav idea needed Serbia more than Serbia needed them. (Yelavich)

A decisive event for the destiny of the South Slavs occurred in April 1915 when Italy joined the Entente. The London Treaty of 26th April 1915 envisaged the reward for Italy in terms of additional territory which the great powers planned to give to the new military ally. Italy was supposed to gain Istria, Dalmatia, and the Adriatic islands. This caused a panic among Croatian, and to a lesser extent Slovenian politicians. They established the Yugoslav Committee on the 30th April 1915, which prompted the Serbian government of Nikola Pasic to speed up the activities for the unification of all South Slavs. Nikola Pasic was in favor of the creation of Greater Serbia, i.e. the unification of all the Serb lands, rather than the creation of the South Slav state. He was supported in his intention by the Imperial Russia. Imperial Russia wanted to satisfy the aspirations of Serbia for the creation of the Greater Serbia, but at the same time urged Serbia to cede the Vardar Macedonia to Bulgaria. Nikola Pasic refused the latter solution, which prompted Bulgaria to enter the war on the side of the Central Powers in late 1915.

Nikola Pasic considered the Yugoslav Committee a concealed the Croatian Committee since it was only preoccupied with the destiny of the Croatian lands. Italian aspirations did concern neither Serbia nor Serbs in Croatia.

There were two events which prompted Nikola Pasic to change his mind. The first one was the February/March Revolution in Russia, which toppled the monarchy. The new government of Alexander Kerensky did not support the creation of the Greater Serbia. Nikola Pasic, therefore, lost the support of the only superpower for his plans. Secondly, at the same time alarming news were delivered to the Serbian government by Nikola Jovanovic and Zivojin Balugdzic, the Serbian envoys in Greece. According to their reports, France and Italy struck a deal to create the Greater Albania under the Italian tutelage after the war, which will comprise Kosovo, the Western Macedonia, and the northern Epirus. All of a sudden, the Serbian lands were threatened in the same way the Croatian lands were threatened by the same enemy, the kingdom of Italy. The Italian Prime Minister Vittorio Emmanuele Orlando openly espoused his hostile attitude towards all South Slavs, advocating a small Serbia, Italian take-over of Dalmatia, and prevention of unification of the South Slavs. Facing the same predicament, the Serbian government and the Yugoslav Committee decided to make a rapprochement, which culminated in the Corfu Declaration of 20th July 1917, which laid the grounds for the future South Slav state. (Sotirovic) It was a common opinion that one strong and united state would be a bulwark against all attempts to appropriate the territories inhabited by the South Slavs. *"A united and vigorous South Slavic state would be created, a state which would be able to defend itself against the Italian pressure. Consequently, the Yugoslav Committee would keep the South Slavic Adriatic littoral in the new state, while Serbia's Government would be in a position to preserve the territories of Western Macedonia and Kosovo-Metohia"* (Sotirovic)

The main impetus for the creation of the common state of the South Slavs was, therefore, the threat of the other races, particularly Italy.

The new South Slavic state lost Istria, the town of Zadar (Zara), and several Adriatic islands to Italy, but gained most of them, Dalmatia, and preserved Kosovo-Metohija and Western Macedonia. Italy was not happy with that arrangement since it fell short of the promises it was given by the London Treaty. The relationship between Yugoslavia and Italy was tense and the war between the two states was barely averted in 1931.

In-spite of all external pressures the territory of the first Yugoslavia was preserved until 1941. By the end of the World War II victorious Partisans increased the territory of Yugoslavia by almost 20,000 km^2, which included the Istria peninsula. From 1945 until the break-up of Yugoslavia in 1991/92 the territory of Yugoslavia, which contained around 17% of non-South Slavs, was preserved. There were occasional attempts of

Bulgaria and Italy to claims their rights on Macedonia, Istria, and parts of Dalmatia. This led to temporary cooling down the relationships between Yugoslavia and the two countries, but nothing serious happened. A high reputation which Yugoslavia enjoyed in the world prompted the international community to condemn such attempts by Bulgaria and Italy.

Yugoslavia, therefore, proved to fulfil its political mission. The best proof for this is if one sees what happened when Yugoslavia ceased to exist in the period 1941-45. Its territory was dismembered. Italy took most of Dalmatia and the Slovenian littoral, Hungary took Vojvodina and Medjimurje, Bulgaria took Macedonia and southeastern Serbia, and Albania took Kosovo.

Economic assessment of Yugoslavia. At the time of its creation Yugoslavia was one of the poorest countries in Europe. There were only five countries in Europe which were less developed than Yugoslavia. Yugoslavia was conspicuously more developed than Albania and Turkey, and only slightly more developed than Bulgaria, Romania, and Portugal.

There were huge regional differences in the level of development within Yugoslavia. Regions which were part of the Austro-Hungarian empire were relatively advanced and their income was approaching the Central European standards. Slovenia, Croatia, Vojvodina, and Bosnia had GDP per capita above the Yugoslav average. Herzegovina, which was part of the Austro-Hungarian empire, but whose economic development was neglected, the province of Sandjak, Montenegro, Kosovo, and Macedonia were quite poor and backward. Serbia, which gained independence in 1878 at the Congress of Berlin, was somewhere in-between, but closer to the former than to the latter.

The First Yugoslavia had neither politically nor economically a fair deal. Circumstances for its economic development were unfavorable. The anemic growth of the Yugoslav economy in the first decade of its existence caused a fall in its GDP per capita index from 41 in 1913 to 31 in 1929 to the Western European average. Data for the 1930s a few and far in between. However, apart from Slovenia all other parts of Yugoslavia were hardly hit by the Great Depression. As a result, some parts, including Bosnia and Herzegovina, recorded a fall in economic activity in a period 1929-38.

The following table shows a rise in GDP for the Second Yugoslavia, its most developed parts, and chosen countries.

Table 26 – GDP levels and growth in Yugoslavia, its most developed parts, and chosen countries 1950-86 (in $ US)

Country	1950	1986	Index
Austria	1,108	9,990	902
Greece	430	3,680	856
Italy	1,022	8,550	856
Japan	591	12,840	2170
Hungary	769	2,020	263
Turkey	389	1,110	286
Yugoslavia	469	2,300	486
Serbia	407	2,075	509
The Serbia Proper	450	2,291	509
Vojvodina	387	2,714	701
Croatia	532	2,873	540
Slovenia	820	4,664	569

SOURCE: Ljubomir Madzar:" Suton socijalističkih privreda – simptomi, uzroci i institucionalne uslovljenosti sloma socijalističlih privreda" (The Eclipse of Socialist Economies-Symptoms, Causes, and Institutional Conditions of the Collapse of Socialist Economies"), Ekonomski institute Beograd 1990, p

The three countries already used for comparison grew faster compared to Yugoslavia. As a result, Austria increased its index to Yugoslavia from 236 in 1950 to 434 in 1986, Italy from 218 in 1950 to 372 in 1986, and Greece from 92 in 1950 to 160 in 1986.

The following table shows growth rates of the most important European countries and Yugoslavia in a period 1950-73.

Table 27 – GDP Per Capita Growth Rates in the Most Important Western European Countries and Yugoslavia 1950-73

Country	GDP PER CAPITA GROWTH RATES 1950-73
Austria	4.94
Belgium	3.55
Denmark	3.08
Finland	4.25
France	4.05
Germany	5.02
Italy	4.95
Netherlands	3.45
Norway	3.19
Sweden	3.07
Switzerland	3.08
United Kingdom	2.44
West Europe	3.93
Yugoslavia	4.49

SOURCE: Angus Maddison, op.cit, p186

Yugoslavia performed fairly well in terms of GDP per capita growth in a period which comprises years 1952-65, which Branko Horvat called "a golden age of the Yugoslav economy" and grew slightly faster than West Europe. This led to a small conversion in terms of GDP per capita.

In the second half of the 1970s the world economy was engulfed in stagflation, which turned into a recession in the beginning of the 1980s. While West Europe recovered in the second half of the 1980s Yugoslavia never got out of woods. The whole decade was lost for the Yugoslav economy and according to one source (Madzar) the growth rate fell to 0.83 per annum, without taking into account a rise in population. Another source (Jackson), estimates that the index per capita for the Yugoslav economy to Western European average fell from 41 in 1913 to 22 in 1992, with one proviso that 1991 and 1992 were the years when wars in Croatia and Bosnia and Herzegovina started.

Some other indicators suggest that the Yugoslav economy did not perform that well even when it achieved high growth rates. According to one study (Sirc) the efficiency of the Yugoslav economy was 30-40% lower compared to Spain, Portugal, and Greece, the countries which were at the similar level of development.

The American economist Charles Kindlerberger analyzed the relationship between the level of economic development and the balance of payments. His research concluded that most of countries pass through four stages: 1. A young debtor, 2. A mature debtor, 3. A young creditor, and 4. A mature creditor. In the early stages of development, the country is predominantly agrarian. Exports of agricultural products is not sufficient to earn enough hard currency to purchase machinery and equipment for industrial growth. The country must borrow money. This is a stage of a young debtor, which is characterized by deficits in the balance of payments and external debt. In the second stage the country built industrial capacities and is able to increase its exports, achieving surplus in the balance of payments. However, this surplus is insufficient to pay off debts accumulated in the first stage. This is the stage of a mature debtor. In the third stage the country increases its surplus in the balance of payments, pays off the debts in the first stage and becomes a net creditor. This is the stage of a young creditor. In the fourth stage the country has aging population. Savings falls, and the country records deficits in the balance of payments. However, the country is still a net creditor. This is the stage of a mature creditor. (Kindlerberger)

In 1967 Yugoslavia reached the level of development at which it should have moved to a stage of a mature debtor. It never happened and Yugoslavia continued to struggle with the balance of payments. The surplus in the balance of payments was achieved only towards the end of 1980s. However, this was the result of extensive use of price and currency dumping, desperately applied to boost exports and obtain hard currency to pay off annuities on external debt rather that a sign of the strength of the Yugoslav economy.

In the 1980s Yugoslavia experienced hyperinflation. Before that inflation was much lower. However, in a period 1965-80 the World Bank estimated that an average rate of inflation in Yugoslavia was 15.3%, among the highest in the world. This caused several devaluations of the Yugoslav dinar.

After Yugoslavia opened its borders in 1965 more than 1 million its citizens, mainly unemployed, left the country. In-spite of this, and artificial employment, which was the characteristic of all the socialist economies (albeit in Yugoslavia it was much lower than in the countries of the Eastern Block), Yugoslavia struggled with a high unemployment. During the 1980s an average rate of unemployment was around 15%, with huge regional differences; 4-5% in Slovenia and 37% in Kosovo.

In conclusion, Yugoslavia was not economically successful, in-spite of some good periods of economic growth.

Cultural assessment of Yugoslavia. Most historians agree that there were three factors which glued Yugoslavia in the interwar period: 1. A threat of other races, 2. A small communist party, and 3. Cultural links based on a similar mentality, and same or similar language. In modern Europe the threat of other races is not present any more. The communist party ceased to exist in 1990. What remained are the cultural links between the Yugoslav nations. These links have been preserved even after the break-up of the country. They are reflected in several fields.

<u>Literary events.</u> Literary events in the successor Yugoslav states gather writers from all parts of the former Yugoslavia. Very often writers from one Yugoslav country receive a prize in another Yugoslav country.

<u>Films, Television series, and theatre.</u> Actors from Serbia and Croatia played in television series in Bosnia and Herzegovina, actors from Bosnia and Herzegovina played in television series in Croatia, Serbian actors played in Croatian television series and vice-versa. Actors from Montenegro played in television series in Serbia and Vice-versa. Co-operation in the film industry produced some brilliant results, such as in the case of the Oscar winning film "No Man's Land", and the highly acclaimed film "Quo Vadis Aida".

<u>Musical festivals and concerts.</u> Musicians very often perform in concerts in other Yugoslav states. Not rarely, musicians from other Yugoslav states are invited to perform at important events such as New Year or some other public holidays. Concerts are frequent and very well attended.

When Yugoslavia was a political community, it was not an economic community. Even when it is not a political community, Yugoslavia is still a cultural community.

In a nutshell, Yugoslavia proved to be a successful political and cultural project, but an unsuccessful economic project.

LITERATURE

"Inflacija u Jugoslaviji bila je ogromna, svet je o tome brujao: čeka li nas opet? (Inflation in Yugoslavia was enormous, the whole world talked about it: are we waiting another one?) (Info biznis) 03/01/22

Amadeo Kimberley: "What is the Gold Standard?", The Balance, August 2021

Anadir Fikret: "Tradition and Rural Change in Southeastern Europe During Ottoman Rule, in Chirot Daniel (ed)": "The origins of Backwardness in Eastern Europe", Berkeley-Los Angeles University of California Press, 1989

Barre Andre: "La Bosnie Herzegovine:Administration Autrichienne de 1878 a 1903", L. Michaud, Paris 1906

Bekavac S, Skenderovic R:" Povijest 3 (History 3), ZAGREB ALFA 2009

Berend Ivan T. and Ranki Gyorgy: "The European Periphery & Industrialization 1780-1914", Cambridge University Press, Printed in Budapest 1982

Bihl Wolfdieter: "Von Der Donaumonarchie zur Zweiten Republik- Daten zur osterreichischen Geschichte seit 1867", Bohlau Verlag Geselschaft, Wien Koln 1989

Bjelica Dimitrije: "Šahovska čitanka", Svjetlost Sarajevo 1973

Brekalo Miljenko & Brekalo Snježana: "Uzroci finansijskog sloma u Socijalističkoj Federativnoj Republici Jugoslaviji", Mostariensia: Časopis za društvene I humanističke znanosti, Vol 22. No.2, 2018

Breuilly: "Austria, Prussia, and Germany 1806-1871, Routledge, UK 2917

Bronza Boro: "Austrijska politika prema prostoru Bosne i Hercegovine, 1699-1788, Filozofski fakultet Banjaluka 2012

Brue Stanley & Grant Randy R.:" "The Evolution of Economic Thought"-eight edition, South Western Cengage Learning, USA 2013

Chirot Daniel (ed): "The origins of Backwardness in Eastern Europe", Berkeley-Los Angeles University of California Press, 1989

Cokorilo Djordje: "Tajna istorija Austrijske politike I njezino produženje u Bosni I Hercegovini", Štamparija Svetozara Nikolića, Beograd 1906

Cvijic Jovan: "L'Annexion la Bosnie et la question Serbe", Libraire Haachettie, Paris 1909

Die Anfange der Demokratischen Bewegung in Osterreich von der Spataufklarung bis zur Revolution 1848/49:Eine Kommentierte Quellenauswahl, Frankfurt am Mein 1999

Domljan Vjekoslav: "Potezanje vitalnog r(n)acionalnog interesa", Lijepa riječ Tuzla 2018

Duikers Jackson William J. & Spielvogel J. :" The Essential World History – Eight edition", Cengage Learning, Canada 2017

Enderink S.W.F. : "Austria and Prussia-German Unification in the nineteenth century", master thesis defended at the university of Utrecht, the Netherlands, 2010

"Gerlach Stefan & Stuart Rebeca:" International Co-Movements of Inflation 1851-1913", Irene Working Paper, N0 21-02, Institute of Economic Research, University of Neuchatel

GLIGOROV VLADIMIR: "Jugoslavija I razvoj, koristi I troškovi ključna tema sporenja"(Jugoslavia and development, benefits and costs, key topic of dispute), in "Jugoslavija u istorijskoj perspektivi" ("Jugoslavia in Historic Perspective"), Helsinki Committee for Serbia, Belgrade 2017

Gross N.T.: "The Habsburg Monarchy 1750-1914", in Carlo M. Cipolla(editor): The Fontana Economic History of Europe-The Emergence of Industrial Societes-1, Collins Clear-Type Press, London and Glasgow, 1973

Harcet Josip, Heinrichs Lorraine, Seiler Palmira Mariz & Skoumal Marienne Torres: "Mathematics Higher Level", Oxford University Press 2012

Hauptmann Ferdinand: "Die Osterreichische-Ungarische Herrschaft in Bosnien und der Hercegovina" 1878-1918. Wirtschafts Politik und Wirtschaftenwickelung, Graz 1983

Henderson: "The Rise of German Industrial Power", University of California, USA 1975

HOARE MARKO ATTILA: "The Bosnian Muslims in the Second World War", Hurst & Company, London 2013

Hoare Marko Attila : "The History of Bosnia-from the Middle Ages to the Present Day", Saqi book, London 2007

Hodžić Kadrija: "Politička ekonomija socijalizma u Bosni I Hercegovini" 8Political Economy of Socialism I Bosnia and Herzegovina), neobjavljeni rukopis

HODZIC KADRIJA: "Tuzlanski procesi", Sarajevo 2021

Horvat Branko: "ABC jugoslavenskog socijalizma", Globus Zagreb 1989

Horvat Branko: "Politička ekonomija socijalizma", Globus Zagreb 1984

Hrelja Kemal: "Industrija Bosne I Hercegovine. do kraja prvog svjetskog rata", Beograd 1961

Imamović Mustafa: "Historija Bošnjaka", BZK Preporod Sarajevo 2006

Imamovic Mustafa: "Historija Bošnjaka", BZK Preporord Sarajevo 2006

Juzbašić Dževad: "Politika i privreda Bosne i Hercegovine pod Austrougarskom upravom",   ANUBiH, Sarajevo 2002

Kapidžić Hamdija: "Austro-ugarska politika u Bosni I Hercegovini I jugoslovensko pitanje za vrijeme Prvog svjetskog rata", Grafički zavod Sarajevo 1958

Kapidzic Hamdija: "Bosna I Hercegovina za vrijeme austrougarske vladavine (1878-1918), Sarajevo 1968

Kasumovic Amila: "Austrougarska trgovinska politika u Bosni I Hercegovini 1878-1914", Udruga za modern povijest, Sarajevo 2016

Kindlerberger Charles: "The International Economics", Homewood Illinois USA 1965

Koetschet Josef: "Osman Pascha, der letzte Grosse Bosnien Vizier und seine Nachfolger", Daniel A Krajon, Sarajevo 1909

Lines David, Marcouse Ian & Martin Barry: "The Complete A-Z BUSINESS STUDIES Handbook", Hodder & Stoughton, UK 1999

Maddison Angus: "The World Economy- Volume 1: The Millennial Perspective, Volume2: Historical Statistics", OECD PUBLISHING 2001

Madzar Ljubomir: "Suton socijalističkih privreda", Institut Ekonomskih Nauka Beograd 1990

Mahmutefendic Tahir: "Economics and Politics-Textbook for Year 3 Grammar School, Social Department", MARKOS BANJALUKA, 2018

Mahmutefendic Tahir: "The Balkans over Years – History and Politics", Xlibris, London 2018

Mahmutefendic Tahir:" Economics and Politics-Textbook for Year 4 Grammar School, Social Department", MARKOS BANJALUKA, 2019

Mahmutefendic Tahir: "Eseji iz apsurdne ekonomije I politike", Bosanska riječ Tuzla, 2014

Mahmutefendić Tahir: "Kratak leksikon ekonomskih pojmova/A Short Lexicon of Economic Concepts", Markos Banjaluka, 2019

Mahmutefendic Tahir: "The Balkans over Years", Xlibris London, 2018

Mahmutefendic Tahir: "The Great Recession, the Balkans, and the Euro, Xlibris London 2015

Malcolm Noel:" Bosna – kratka povijest, Buybook, Sarajevo 2011

Markovic Slobodan: "The Political and Economic Heritage of Modern Serbia: two Centuries of Convergence and Divergence between Serbia and Western Europe", in S.G. Markovich, E.B. Weaver, V. Pavlovic (editors), Challenges to New Democracies in the Balkans, Cigoja Press, Belgrade 2004

MARX & ENGELS CELEBRABAN LAS CONQUISTAS DEL IMPERIALISMO ANGLOSAJON (Marx and Engels Celebrated the Anglo-Saxon Imperialist Conquests), http://juventudnacional-min.blogspot.co.uk 2001_08_01 archie.html

Mirkovic Mijo: "Glavni uzroci gospodarske zaostalosti slavenskih Naroda" (The Main Causes of Economic Backwardness of the Slavic Nations), Dom I Svijet Zagreb 2008

Okey Robin: "Taming Balkan Nationalism" The Habsburg 'Civilizing Mission' in Bosnia", 1878-1914", Oxford University Press 2007

Okey Robin: "The Habsburg Monarchy c 1765-1918", Routledge, Taylor and Francis, Hoboken 2014

Owen J, Haese R, Haese S, Bruce M: "Mathematics for International Student/Mathematics SL ", Haese & Harris Publications, Australia 2007

Palairet Michael: "Economic Development in the Balkan Countries 1800 - 1914 Evolution without Development", Cambridge University Press 1997

Paris B.A "The Prisoner", Hodder & Stoughton", UK 2022

Petrakos George and Totev Stoyan (editors):" The Development of the Balkan Region", Ashgate Publishing Company Limited, 2001

Prelog Milan: "Repetitorij Povijesti Austrougarske Monarhije", Sarajevoer Tagblatt, Sarajevo 1906

RAMET SABRINA: "Nationalism and Federalism in Yugoslavia, 1962 to 1991-Second Edition", Indiana University Press, USA 1992

Redzic Enver (urednik): "Prilozi za istoriju Bosne I Hercegovine, ANUBiH Sarajevo 2006

Rostow W. W.: "The Stages of Economic Growth- A non-communist manifesto", Cambridge University Press 1990

Rostow W. W.: "The World Economy", Macmillan, London 1978

Ruthner et al(ed): "The Political Social and Cultural Impact of the Austro-Hungarian Occupation of Bosnia and Herzegovina, 1878-1918", New York, Peter Lang 2008

Schlomlich & Meisen: "Logaritamske tablice", Zagreb 1972

Schmid Ferdinand: "Bosnien und die Herzegovina unter der Verwaltung Oesterreich-Ungarn", Leipzieg 1914

Schollers Peter (ed): "Real Wages in 19th and 20th Century Europe- Historical and Comparative Perspectives", Berg Publishers Limited, USA 1989

Sirc Ljubo:"Da li je kritika samoupravljanja još uvijek aktuelna?" (Is the Critic of Self-management still up-to-date?), Institut Ekonomskih Nauka Beograd I Centar za Post-komunističke studije London, 1997

Sotirovic Vladislav: "The 1917 Corfu Declaration and its Importance for the Creation of the Kingdom of Serbs, Croats and Slovenes in 1918", The South Slav Journal, Vol 33, No. 1-2, Spring 2014

Sugar Peter: "Industrialization of Bosnia and Herzegovina1978-1918", Washington University Press, Seattle 1963

Taylor Alen J.P.: "Habsburška monarhija", Clio Beograd 2001

Todaro Michael P. & Smith Stephen S. :"Ekonomski razvoj, deveto izdanje", Šahinpašić, Sarajevo 2006

Veber Maks: "Protestantska etika I duh kapitalizma" (The Protestant Ethics and the Spirit of Capitalism), Veselin Maslesa Sarajevo 1972

Von Brachelli Hugo Franz:"Statistische Skizze des norddeutschen Bundes", Leipzig 1868

Wall Nancy: "The Complete A-Z ECONOMICS Handbook", Hodder & Stoughton, UK 2001

Welfens Paul: "Stabilizing and Integrating the Balkans- Economic Analysis of the Stability pact, EU Reforms and International Organizations, Springer 2001

Yelavich Charles and Baebara: "The Establishment of the Balkan National States 1804 – 1920", Washington University Press 1977

Younis Hana: "Svakodnevni život u Sarajevu u doba Topal Osman-paše (1861-1869), magistarski rad, Sarajevo 2006

www.ingramcontent.com/pod-product-compliance
Lightning Source LLC
LaVergne TN
LVHW010201070526
838199LV00062B/4445